U.S. Naval Aviation
A Military Photo Logbook
Volume 1

COMPILED BY
DENNIS R. JENKINS

specialtypress
PUBLISHERS AND WHOLESALERS

ISBN 978-1-58007-114-7

Item Number SP114

PUBLISHERS AND WHOLESALERS

39966 Grand Avenue
North Branch, MN 55056 USA
(651) 277-1400 or (800) 895-4585
www.specialtypress.com

Printed in China

Distributed in the UK and Europe by:

Midland Publishing
4 Watling Drive
Hinckley LE10 3EY, England
Tel: 01455 233 747 Fax: 01455 233 737
www.midlandcountiessuperstore.com

On the Cover, Top Left: *15 October 2006, Arabian Sea – An F/A-18C Hornet assigned to the "Knighthawks" of VFA-136 tests its flare countermeasure system before heading into Afghanistan on a close air support mission after launching from the nuclear-powered aircraft carrier USS Enterprise (CVN 65).* (U.S. Navy photo by Lt. Peter Scheu)

On the Cover, Top Right: *19 October 2006, Atlantic Ocean – A C-2A Greyhound assigned to the "Rawhides" of VRC-40 makes an arrested landing aboard the nuclear-powered aircraft carrier USS Theodore Roosevelt (CVN 71).* (U.S. Navy photo by Mass Communication Specialist 3rd Class Nathan Laird)

On the Cover, Bottom Left: *14 October 2006, San Diego, California – Two CH-46 Sea Knights demonstrate how a Marine Air-Ground Task Force responds when called upon during the Miramar Air show.* (U.S. Marine Corps photo by Lance Cpl. Kelly R. Chase)

On the Cover, Bottom Right: *23 October 2006, Mediterranean Sea – Lt. Kimball Terres, a "shooter" aboard the USS Dwight D. Eisenhower (CVN 69), checks the flight deck's crosswind gages before launching an EA-6B Prowler from VAQ-140.* (U.S. Navy photo by Mass Communication Specialist 2nd Class Miguel Angel Contreras)

On the Back Cover, Upper Right: *06 January 2006, Persian Gulf – Aviation ordnancemen transport an AGM-65 Maverick laser-guided missile after off-loading it from an F/A-18C Hornet aboard the Nimitz-class aircraft carrier USS Theodore Roosevelt (CVN 71).* (U.S. Navy photo by Photographer's Mate Airman Apprentice Nathan Laird)

On the Back Cover, Lower Left: *07 February 2006, Persian Gulf – An F-14D Tomcat from the "Black Lions" of VF-213 prepares to launch from the USS Theodore Roosevelt (CVN 71).* (U.S. Navy photo by Photographer's Mate Airman Derek Allen)

On the Back Cover, Lower Right: *25 March 2006, Al Taqaddum, Iraq – Lance Cpl. Micah E. Vogen, with Marine Light Attack Helicopter Squadron 369, safes a AH-1W Super Cobra's M197 20mm automatic gun after the helicopter returns from a mission.* (U.S. Marine Corps photo by Cpl. Jonathan K. Teslevich)

On the Title Page: *17 January 2006, Pacific Ocean – An F/A-18C Hornet assigned to the "Fighting Vigilantes" of VFA-151 launches from the USS Abraham Lincoln (CVN-72).* (U.S. Navy photo by Photographer's Mate Airman Geoffrey Lewis)

CONTENTS

INTRODUCTION

Three United States military services wear the "Wings of Gold:" Navy, Marines Corps, and Coast Guard. The Navy ordered its first airplane on 8 May 1911 and self-taught flier Eugene Ely, wearing a football helmet and bicycle tube as a life preserver, became the first man to both take off and land on the deck of a ship. Over the following nine decades, Naval Aviation has served the United States in times of peace and war wherever on the globe it was needed. The most widely recognized part of Naval Aviation is undoubtedly operations off the aircraft carriers operated by the U.S. Navy, but naval aircraft operate from a wide variety of shore bases also. Many of these are in Allied nations, not the United States.

Like all organizations, the Navy likes to record its accomplishments, and employs a large team of professional photographers as well as many amateurs. These photographers have few restrictions placed on them about what or when they shoot (although many photographs are never released due to security concerns). The images they capture tend to concentrate on people and events because that is the essence of any organization. Nevertheless, the hardware gets its fair share of exposure, and that is the emphasis of this book.

Military photographers or service members took the photographs contained herein and show Naval Aviation as it exists, in its glory and its sadness, in peace and at war. The captions are edited versions of what the photographer wrote – sometimes I would have emphasized a different aspect of the photograph, but it was not my choice. Often the photographs exist in a vacuum, with little context – there might be a detail shot of a piece of nose art or a weapon with no corresponding overall photo of the aircraft. This is how the Navy released the photo.

The year 2006 saw several milestones in Naval Aviation. These included the retirement of the last Grumman F-14 Tomcats after more than 30 years of first-line service to the fleet. Oddly, given its strictly anti-air beginnings, the Tomcat ended its days as the Navy's premiere ground-attack/strike aircraft. As the old guard was retiring, however, two new aircraft were accepted into service. The Bell Boeing V-22 Osprey finally began arriving at operational units after a particularly grueling development cycle, and the first Boeing EA-18G Growler entered operational testing. This electronic warfare variant of the Super Hornet will eventually replace the venerable Northrop Grumman EA-6B Prowler in Navy, but not Marine Corps, service.

The photographs run the gamut from exciting, action-filled shots of Mach 2 fighters, to pictures of supplies waiting to be loaded onto a transport aircraft. Fighters dropping weapons, and helicopters rescuing stranded people. Aircraft fresh off the assembly line, and ones older than most of the people who read this book. Allies are represented when they participated in joint operations or exercises.

The 300-plus photographs represent a cross-section of Naval Aviation and what it accomplished during 2006. The photographs are presented in roughly chronological order (a few liberties were taken to allow a clean layout for the book) and attempt to show a balanced view, but that is for the reader to ultimately decide.

Dennis R. Jenkins
Cape Canaveral, Florida

02 January 2006, Persian Gulf – A C-2A Greyhound assigned to the "Rawhides" of VRC-40 moves into launching position during pre-flight operations aboard the Nimitz-class aircraft carrier USS Theodore Roosevelt (CVN 71). Roosevelt and her embarked Carrier Air Wing Eight (CVW-8) are underway on a regularly scheduled deployment conducting maritime security operations. (U.S. Navy photo by Photographer's Mate Airman Javier Capella)

01 January 2006, MCAS Yuma, Arizona – A CH-46 Sea Knight with the "Red Dragons" of HMM-268 touches down after an aerial gunnery flight during Exercise Desert Talon 1-06, designed to prepare Marine aviation units for their upcoming deployment to Iraq. (U.S. Marine Corps photo Cpl. Jonathan K. Teslevich)

03 January 2006, Al Asad, Iraq – Major William R. Sauerland, a pilot with the "Bulldogs" of VMA-223 taxis his Boeing AV-8B Harrier after completing a combat mission in Southwest Asia. The Bulldogs deployed to Al Asad from their home at Marine Corps Air Station Cherry Point, North Carolina, during August 2005. (U.S. Marine Corps photo by Cpl. Micah Snead)

09 January 2006, Persian Gulf – An F/A-18 Hornet assigned to the "Golden Warriors" of VFA-87 makes an arrested landing aboard the Nimitz-class aircraft carrier USS Theodore Roosevelt (CVN 71). (U.S. Navy photo by Photographer's Mate Airman Javier Capella)

05 January 2006, MCAS New River, North Carolina – Marines from the future "Thunder Chickens" of VMM-263 perform a "fit-check" of a new Bell V-22 Osprey in their hangar. (U.S. Marine Corps photo by Lance Cpl. Samuel D. White)

06 January 2006, Pacific Ocean – Commander, Carrier Air Wing Fourteen (CVW-14), Capt. Craig Williams, lands an F/A-18E Super Hornet assigned to the "Fighting Redcocks" of VFA-22 on the USS Ronald Reagan (CVN 76). This is the maiden deployment for the Navy's newest nuclear-powered aircraft carrier. (U.S. Navy photo by Photographer's Mate Airman Gary Prill)

06 January 2006, Persian Gulf – An F-14 Tomcat assigned to the "Tomcatters" of VF-31 launches from the waist catapult on the USS Theodore Roosevelt (CVN 71) to provide close-air support to coalition troops in contact with anti-Iraqi forces. (U.S. Navy photo by Photographer's Mate 3rd Class Eben Boothby)

06 January 2006, Pacific Ocean – Damage Controlman (Fireman) Shea Engman collects samples of Aqueous Film Forming Foam (AFFF) on the flight deck aboard USS Nimitz (CVN 68) while preparing for Inspection and Survey. (U.S. Navy photo by Photographer's Mate Airman Melissa Vanderwyst)

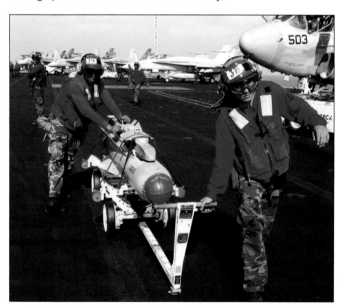

06 January 2006, Persian Gulf – Aviation ordnancemen transport an AGM-65 Maverick laser-guided missile after off-loading it from an F/A-18C Hornet aboard the Nimitz-class aircraft carrier USS Theodore Roosevelt (CVN 71). (U.S. Navy photo by Photographer's Mate Airman Apprentice Nathan Laird)

06 January 2006, Pacific Ocean – Crew members move an emergency heavy lift crane, "Tilly," after lighting off the Aqueous Film Forming Foam (AFFF) system on the flight deck aboard the USS Nimitz (CVN 68) while preparing for Inspection and Survey. (U.S. Navy photo by Photographer's Mate Airman Melissa Vanderwyst)

10 January 2006, Al Asad Airfield, Iraq – Corporal Joseph W. Custalow with VMM-261 (Reinforced), the aviation combat element of the 22nd Marine Expeditionary Unit (Special Operations Capable), secures the rotors of an AH-1W Super Cobra attack helicopter after a mission over Al Anbar province. (U.S. Marine Corps photo by Sgt Richard D. Stephens)

12 January 2006, Persian Gulf – An F/A-18C Hornet launches from the aircraft carrier USS Theodore Roosevelt (CVN 71). Roosevelt and embarked Carrier Air Wing Eight (CVW-8) are currently underway on a regularly scheduled deployment conducting maritime security operations. (U.S. Navy photo by Photographer's Mate 3rd Class Eben Boothby)

11 January 2006, Camp Lejeune, North Carolina – A Marine attaches the single-point refueling rig to a Bell AH-1W Super Cobra attack helicopter at Landing Zone Bluebird. (U.S. Marine Corps photo by: Lance Cpl. Samuel D. White)

11 January 2006, Camp Lejeune, North Carolina – Marines from MALS-29 load 5-inch rockets onto a Bell AH-1W Super Cobra. An AGM-114 Hellfire missile is on the outboard weapons station. (U.S. Marine Corps photo by: Lance Cpl. Jeffrey A. Cosola)

12 January 2006, Persian Gulf – An S-3B Viking prepares to launch from the USS Theodore Roosevelt (CVN 71). Note the ram air turbine (RAT) on the nose of the refueling store under the left wing. (U.S. Navy photo by Photographer's Mate 3rd Class Eben Boothby)

12 January 2006, Persian Gulf – Flight deck handlers direct an F-14D Tomcat assigned to the "Tomcatters" of VF-31 into launch position aboard the USS Theodore Roosevelt (CVN 71). (U.S. Navy photo by Photographer's Mate Airman Apprentice Nathan Laird)

15 January 2006, Sigonella, Sicily – Three P-3C Orion aircraft belonging to the "Tridents" of VP-26 stand ready on a rain-soaked airfield. Originally designed as a land-based, long-range, anti-submarine warfare (ASW) patrol aircraft, the P-3C's mission has evolved to include sur- veillance of the battlespace, either at sea or over land. (U.S. Navy photo by Photographer's Mate 1st Class John Collins)

12 January 2006, Pacific Ocean – An HH-60H Seahawk assigned to the "Black Knights" of HS-4 takes part in an anti-submarine warfare exercise off the coast of Hawaii. Theis Seahawk is deployed aboard the USS Ronald Reagan (CVN 76). (U.S. Navy photo by Chief Journalist Donnie W. Ryan)

15 January 2006, Al Taqqadum, Iraq – Artwork on a CH-46 Sea Knight indicates the number of years Marine Medium Helicopter Squadron 161 has been active. HMM-161 has seen combat in every major conflict that the Marine Corps has been involved with since the Korean War. (U.S. Marine Corps photo by Cpl. Cullen J. Tiernan)

13 January 2006, Atlantic Ocean – Flight deck crew aboard the amphibious assault ship USS Bataan (LHD 5) brace themselves as an MH-53E Sea Dragon assigned to the "Vanguard" of HM-14 lands. (U.S. Navy photo by Photographer's Mate 3rd Class Jeremy L. Grisham)

16 January 2006, Persian Gulf – An F-14D Tomcat assigned to the "Tomcatters" of VF-31 lands aboard the nuclear-powered Nimitz-class aircraft carrier USS Theodore Roosevelt (CVN 71). (U.S. Navy photo by Photographer's Mate Airman Sheldon Rowley)

16 January 2006, Pacific Ocean – An F/A-18C Hornet assigned to the "Kestrels" of VFA-137 performs a touch-and-go aboard the USS Abraham Lincoln (CVN 72) off the coast of Southern California. (U.S. Navy photo by Photographer's Mate 2nd Class Seth C. Peterson)

17 January 2006, Pacific Ocean – An F/A-18C Hornet assigned to the "Fighting Vigilantes" of VFA-151 launches from the USS Abraham Lincoln (CVN 72) off the coast of Southern California. (U.S. Navy photo by Photographer's Mate Airman Geoffrey Lewis)

18 January 2006, Persian Gulf – An F/A-18C Hornet launches from the flight deck aboard the nuclear-powered Nimitz-class aircraft carrier USS Theodore Roosevelt (CVN 71). (U.S. Navy photo by Photographer's Mate Airman Javier Capella)

18 January 2006, MCB Hawaii, Kaneohe Bay – A LITENING laser designator pod mounted under a Boeing F/A-18A+ Hornet, assigned to the "Cowboys" of VFMA-112. (U.S. Marine Corps photo by Sgt. Joel A. Chaverri)

19 January 2006, Al Asad, Iraq – Brigadier Gen. R. David Papak, the commanding general of 4th Marine Aircraft Wing, and Lt. Col. Leo Kilgore, commanding officer of HMM-774, prepare for a mission in a CH-46 Sea Knight. (U.S. Marine Corps photo by Cpl. Micah Snead)

17 January 2006, Atlantic Ocean – An RQ-8A Fire Scout, the air vehicle part of the Vertical Takeoff and Landing Tactical Unmanned Aerial Vehicle (VTUAV) system, prepares for the first autonomous landing aboard the amphibious transport dock ship USS Nashville (LPD 13). With an on-station endurance of more than four hours, the Fire Scout is capable of providing coverage at 110 nautical miles from the launch site. Using a baseline payload that includes electro-optical/infrared sensors and a laser rangefinder/designator, Fire Scout can find and identify tactical targets, track and designate targets, accurately provide targeting data to strike platforms, employ precision weapons, and perform battle damage assessment. (U.S. Navy photo by Kurt Lengfield)

21 January 2006, Atlantic City, New Jersey – An HH-65C Dolphin flies low over the Atlantic Ocean. The newly re-engined "Charlie" model helicopters are part of the Coast Guard's Deepwater program. (U.S. Coast Guard photo by PA2 John Edwards)

22 January 2006, Atsugi, Japan – Airman Eric Bobadilla sweeps snow off the back of a Boeing F/A-18F Super Hornet assigned to the "Diamondbacks" of VFA-102. (U.S. Navy photo by Photographer's Mate Airman Jonathan D. Chandler)

23 January 2006, Pacific Ocean – Marines aboard the amphibious assault ship USS Peleliu (LHA 5) maintain an AV-8B Harrier assigned to the "Blacksheep" of VMFA-214. Peleliu and Expeditionary Strike Group Three are underway off the coast of Southern California conducting their Joint Task Force Exercise in preparation for an upcoming deployment. (U.S. Navy photo by Photographer's Mate 3rd Class Nathaniel J. Karl)

25 January 2006, Atlantic Ocean – A T-45C Goshawk, makes an arrested landing aboard the USS Dwight D. Eisenhower (CVN 69) during carrier qualifications with student Naval aviators. (U.S. Navy photo by Photographer's Mate Airman Dale Miller)

25 January 2006, Atlantic Ocean – A Sailor moves away from a C-2A Greyhound assigned to the "Rawhides" of VRC-40 after hooking it up to a catapult on the USS Dwight D. Eisenhower (CVN 69). (U.S. Navy photo by Photographer's Mate 3rd Class Christopher B. Long)

27 January 2006, Norfolk, Virginia – One of the last two H-3 Sea Kings from the "Fleet Angels" of HSC-2 making its final flight before being replaced by an MH-60S Seahawk. (U.S. Navy photo by Photographer's Mate Airman Tristan Miller)

26 January 2006, Sigonella, Sicily – Aviation Structural Mechanic 3rd Class Steve Hastey assigned to the "Tridents" of VP-26, conducts routine maintenance on a P-3C Orion. VP-26 is currently deployed to Naval Air Station Sigonella in support of Operation Iraqi Freedom and maritime patrols. (U.S. Navy photo by Photographer's Mate 2nd Class Johnathan Roark)

29 January 2006, Al Qaim, Iraq – Darrin Wagoner, right, a contractor working for the Marine Corps explains to Secretary of the Navy Donald C. Winter the operation and capabilities of the Scan Eagle unmanned aerial vehicle (U.S. Navy photo by Chief Journalist Craig P. Strawser)

29 January 2006, Northern Marianas Islands – Crew chiefs from HMM-262 (Reinforced) load fuel into their UH-1N Huey from a forward arming and refueling point on the island of Tinian. (U.S. Marine Corps photo by Cpl Will Lathrop)

06 February 2006, Persian Gulf – Helicopter crews from Carrier Air Wing Eight (CVW-8) relieve each other on the flight deck of the USS Theodore Roosevelt (CVN 71). (U.S. Navy photo by Photographer's Mate 3rd Class Michael D. Cole)

07 February 2006, Persian Gulf – An F-14D Tomcat assigned to the "Tomcatters" of VF-31 is launched from the USS Theodore Roosevelt (CVN 71). The Tomcatters and Black Lions of VF-213 (see facing page) are the last active squadrons flying F-14s. (U.S. Navy photo by Photographer's Mate 3rd Class Michael D. Cole)

07 February 2006, Persian Gulf – An F-14D Tomcat from the "Black Lions" of VF-213 is directed to a steam-powered catapult prior to launch from the USS Theodore Roosevelt (CVN 71). (U.S. Navy photo by Photographer's Mate 3rd Class Michael D. Cole)

07 February 2006, Persian Gulf – Night operations with an F-14D Tomcat from the "Tomcatters" of VF-31 aboard the USS Theodore Roosevelt (CVN 71). (U.S. Navy photo by Photographer's Mate Airman Apprentice Nathan Laird)

07 February 2006, Persian Gulf – An F-14D Tomcat from the "Black Lions" of VF-213 prepares to launch from the Nimitz-class aircraft carrier USS Theodore Roosevelt (CVN 71). Roosevelt and embarked Carrier Air Wing Eight (CVW-8) are currently underway on a regularly scheduled deployment conducting maritime security operations. (U.S. Navy photo by Photographer's Mate Airman Derek Allen)

08 February 2006, Pacific Ocean – An F/A-18C Hornet assigned to the "Death Rattlers" of VMFA-323 launches from the USS John C. Stennis (CVN 74) off the coast of Southern California. (U.S. Navy photo by Photographer's Mate 3rd Class Ryan J. Restvedt)

11 February 2006, Pacific Ocean– Aviation Ordnanceman Airman Robert Van Auken prepares to move Mk-82/BLU-111 general-purpose bombs aboard the USS John C. Stennis (CVN 74). (U.S. Navy photo by Airman Alan Willis)

09 February 2006, New Orleans, Louisiana – A Coast Guard Air Station New Orleans air crew flies over downtown New Orleans in one of the unit's new HH-65C rescue helicopters. The "Charlie" models feature new, more powerful engines that provide substantial power, flight control, and flight safety improvements. (U.S. Coast Guard photo by PA1 Kyle Niemi)

11 February 2006, McKinleyville, California – A HH-65 from Air Station Humboldt Bay suffered a mishap and crashed in the surf near Samoa Beach, due west of Eureka. The crew was responding to a capsized boat with four persons in the water. The crew escaped without injury and continued with the rescue mission. (U.S. Coast Guard photo by Lt. Shawn Geraghty)

11 February 2006, Pacific Ocean – An MH-60S Seahawk assigned to the "Black Jacks" of HSC-21 transports ammunition from the aircraft carrier USS Nimitz (CVN 68) to the fast combat support ship USNS Bridge (T-AOE 10). Nimitz is currently preparing for a major propulsion plant examination off the coast of Southern California. (U.S. Navy photo by Photographer's Mate Airman Melissa Vanderwyst)

09 February 2006, Al Asad, Iraq – Lance Cpl. Chris L. Switzer directs a taxiing F/A-18D Hornet belonging to the "Hawks" from Marine All Weather Fighter Attack Squadron 553 (VMFA(AW)-533) of Marine Aircraft Group 16 (Reinforced), 3rd Marine Aircraft Wing. The Hawks assumed responsibility for providing close air support to friendly forces in Iraq from VMFA(AW)-332, MAG-31, 2nd MAW less than 24 hours after their arrival. (U.S. Marine Corps photo by Cpl. Jonathan K. Teslevich)

13 February 2006, Persian Gulf – Two F-14D Tomcats make departures aboard USS Theodore Roosevelt (CVN 71). The nuclear powered aircraft carrier is currently underway on a regularly scheduled deployment supporting maritime security operations. Notice how the right-hand aircraft is banking away to ensure safe separation from the other catapults. (U.S. Navy photo by Photographer's Mate Airman Javier Capella)

13 February 2006, Red Sea – An F-14D Tomcat assigned to the "Black Lions" of VF-213 launches from the USS Theodore Roosevelt (CVN 71) while an F/A-18 waits its turn. (U.S. Navy photo by Photographer's Mate Airman Javier Capella)

15 February 2006, in the Suez Canal – The USS Theodore Roosevelt (CVN 71) passes under the Friendship Bridge during the ship's transit through the Suez Canal. (U.S. Navy photo by Photographer's Mate Airman Apprentice Nathan Laird)

14 February 2006, Philippine Sea – Combat Cargo Marines brace themselves as an MH-60S Seahawk lands on the flight deck of the amphibious dock landing ship USS Harpers Ferry (LSD 49). Harpers Ferry is part of the three-ship, Sasebo, Japan-based Forward Deployed Amphibious Ready Group that also includes USS Essex (LHD 2) and USS Juneau (LPD 10). (U.S. Navy photo by Journalist 2nd Class Brian P. Biller)

16 February 2006, Atlantic Ocean – An F/A-18 Super Hornet prepares to launch from the USS Dwight D. Eisenhower (CVN 69) during the Tailored Ship's Training Availability/Final Evaluation Period. (U.S. Navy photo by Lithographer 1st Class Patrick Gould)

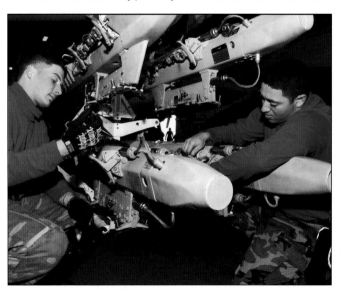

16 February 2006, Atlantic Ocean – Aviation ordnancemen John Boyd and Adin Carrillo from the "Jolly Rogers" of VFA-103 work on a bomb rack aboard the USS Dwight D. Eisenhower (CVN 69). (U.S. Navy photo by Photographer's Mate 3rd Class Andrew Geraci)

19 February 2006, Indian Ocean – Aviation ordnancemen assigned to the "Fist of the Fleet" of VFA-25 perform a post-fire check on an M61A1 20mm cannon from an F/A-18 Hornet in the hangar bay aboard the USS Ronald Reagan (CVN 76). (U.S. Navy photo by Illustrator Draftsman Seaman Jack McCann)

19 February 2006, Saint Bernard, Philippines – A CH-46E Sea Knight from the "Flying Tigers" of HMM-262 takes off after unloading food, blankets, water, and other vital supplies to survivors of the devastating landslide. (U.S. Navy Photo by Photographer's Mate 1st Class Michael D. Kennedy)

25 February 2006, NAS Oceana, Virginia – An AV-8B Harrier undergoes maintenance in the transient hangar while CH-53E Super Stallions from the "Blue Knights" of HMM-365 (Reinforced) sit outside. (U.S. Marine Corps photo by Lance Cpl. Jeffrey A. Cosola)

25 February 2006, Philippine Sea – An SH-60S Seahawk from the "Island Knights" of HCS-25 maneuvers over the flight deck of the fleet replenishment oiler USNS Yukon (T-AO 202). (U.S. Navy photo by Journalist 2nd Class Brian P. Biller)

22 February 2006, Persian Gulf – Flight deck personnel perform a final pre-flight check of an E-2C Hawkeye assigned to the "Black Eagles" of VAW-113 aboard the USS Ronald Reagan (CVN 76). (U.S. Navy photo by Photographer's Mate 3rd Class Christopher D. Blachly)

23 February 2006, Al Asad, Iraq – Cpl. John M. Pruett inspects the rear of a CH-46 Sea Knight assigned to the "Wild Goose" of HMM-774 as the helicopter begins to power down. (U.S. Marine Corps photo by Lance Cpl. James B. Hoke)

27 February 2006, Atlantic Ocean – Sailors stationed aboard the USS Dwight D. Eisenhower (CVN 69) give a pre-launch thumbs up for a C-2A Greyhound assigned to the "Rawhides" of VRC-40. (U.S. Navy photo by Photographer's Mate 3rd Class Christopher B. Long)

26 February 2006, Boston, Massachusetts – An Agusta MH-68A Stingray short-range armed interdiction helicopter sits aboard the Coast Guard Cutter Escanaba (WMEC 907). The helicopter is equipped with a 7.62mm machine gun used for warning shots and suppression fire, and a 0.50-caliber sniper rifle employed to disable go-fast boat engines. (U.S. Coast Guard photo by PA2 Lisa Hennings)

03 March 2006, San Diego, California – Pilots assigned to the "Saberhawks" of HSL-47 prepare for takeoff in four SH-60B Seahawks to join the Carrier Strike Group led by the Nimitz-class aircraft carrier USS Abraham Lincoln (CVN 72). Lincoln and embarked Carrier Air Wing Two (CVW-2) are beginning a six-month deployment. (U.S. Navy photo by Journalist Seaman Jennifer Kimball)

27 February 2006, Atlantic Ocean – An E-2C Hawkeye assigned to the "Tigertails" of VAW-125 lands aboard the USS Dwight D. Eisenhower (CVN 69). (U.S. Navy photo by Photographer's Mate 3rd Class Christopher B. Long)

01 March 2006, Al Asad, Iraq – An AV-8B Harrier taxies before a mission. Marine Aircraft Group 16 (Reinforced) is responsible for aerial support to ground forces throughout Iraq. (U.S. Marine Corps photo by Cpl. Jonathan K. Teslevich)

04 March 2006, Atlantic Ocean – An E-2C Hawkeye assigned to the "Tigertails" of VAW-125 taxis aboard the USS Dwight D. Eisenhower (CVN 69) during the Tailored Ship's Training Availability/Final Evaluation Period. (U.S. Navy photo by Lithographer 3rd Class Sharay Bennett)

28 February 2006, MCAS Futenma, Okinawa – A CH-46E Sea Knight with the "Dragons" of HMM-265 lands on the live-fire range on Kumejima to drop off Marines with the 5th Air Naval Gunfire Liaison Company. (U.S. Marine Corps photo by Lance Cpl. Kamran Sadaghiani)

06 March 2006, Washington, DC – The Vertical Unmanned Aerial Vehicle (VUAV) is a short-range unmanned tilt-rotor that will allow the Coast Guard to extend the surveillance capability of its major cutters. (U.S. Coast Guard photo courtesy of Northrop Grumman)

06 March 2006, Atlantic Ocean – Sailors aboard the fast combat support ship USNS Supply (T-AOE-6) connect a lifting cable to an MH-60S Seahawk assigned to the "Dragon Whales" of HSC-28 to transfer ammunition to the USS George Washington (CVN 73). (U.S. Navy photo by Photographer's Mate Airman Joshua Olson)

07 March 2006, Atlantic Ocean – Sailors assigned to the "Checkmates" of VFA-211 maintain the M61A2 20mm cannon on an F/A-18F Super Hornet in the hangar bay of the USS Enterprise (CVN 65) during a Composite Training Unit Exercise. (U.S. Navy photo by Photographer's Mate 2nd Class Milosz Reterski)

03 March 2006, Atlantic Ocean – Photographer's Mate 3rd Class Rob Gaston takes photographs from an MH-60S assigned to the "Dragon Whales" of HSC-28. (U.S. Navy photo by Photographer's Mate Airman Devonte Jones)

07 March 2006, Manama, Bahrain – Personnel assigned to the "Blackhawks" of HM-15 load cargo into a Sikorsky MH-53E Sea Dragon prior to a mission. (U.S. Navy photo by Photographer's Mate 2nd Class Michael J. Sandberg)

08 March 2006, Persian Gulf – Marines from Company C, 1st Battalion, 4th Marine Regiment, 11th Marine Expeditionary Unit, (Special Operations Capable) fast rope from a CH-46 Sea Knight assigned to the "SeaElk" of HMM-166 to the deck of the USS Peleliu (LHA-5) during a training exercise. (U.S. Navy photo by Lt. Vincent T. Stanley)

10 March 2006, Honolulu, Hawaii – An aviation maintenance technician from Coast Guard Air Station Barbers Point on the island of Oahu, Hawaii, practices a basket drop and recovery with a small boat. (U.S. Coast Guard photo by PA2 Brooksann Anderson)

10 March 2006, Atlantic Ocean – F/A-18 Hornets assigned to the "Valions" of VFA-15 prepare to launch from the USS Theodore Roosevelt (CVN 71) during a six-month deployment. (U.S. Navy photo by Photographer's Mate Airman Javier Capella)

10 March 2006, Atlantic Ocean – An F/A-18C Hornet assigned to the "Golden Warriors" of VFA-87 launches from the USS Theodore Roosevelt (CVN 71). VFA-87 is departing the ship and returning to its home port of Naval Air Station Oceana as Roosevelt and Carrier Air Wing Eight return from a deployment. (U.S. Navy photo by Lithographer 3rd Class Jonathan Snyder)

10 March 2006, Atlantic Ocean – An F-14D Tomcat assigned to the "Tomcatters" of VF-31 launches from the USS Theodore Roosevelt (CVN 71) completing its final deployment flying the F-14. (U.S. Navy photo by Photographer's Mate Airman Javier Capella)

10 March 2006, Virginia Beach, Virginia – Twenty-two F-14D Tomcats from VF-31 and VF-213 conduct a flyover of NAS Oceana after completing their final deployment with the F-14 Tomcat. (U.S. Navy photo by Photographer's Mate 3rd class Christopher J. Garcia)

10 March 2006, Pacific Ocean – A crew member from the "Golden Falcons" of HS-2 conducts a preflight check on the tail rotor of an SH-60F Seahawk aboard the USS Abraham Lincoln (CVN 72). (U.S. Navy photo by Photographer's Mate Airman James R. Evans)

14 March 2006, MCAS Cherry Point, North Carolina – Cpl. Jared S. Kinnaman, an ordnance technician with the "Tigers" of VMA-542, performs maintenance on a LITENING pod from an AV-8B Harrier. (U.S. Marine Corps photo by Cpl. J. R. Stence)

13 March 2006, Pacific Ocean – An F/A-18C Hornet assigned to the "Rough Raiders" of VFA-125 launches from the USS John C. Stennis (CVN 74) off the coast of Southern California. (U.S. Navy photo by Photographer's Mate 2nd Class Mark J. Rebilas)

15 March 2006, Manama, Bahrain – Pilots assigned to the "Blackhawks" of HM-15 monitor gauges on the console of an MH-53E Sea Dragon as they perform start-up procedures. (U.S. Navy Photo by Photographer's Mate 2nd Class Michael J. Sandberg)

21 March 2006, Korean Straits – An Army CH-47 Chinook of Bravo Company, 2-52nd Aviation Regiment, the "Innkeepers," lands aboard USS Blue Ridge (LCC 19) during a joint Navy-Army exercise. (U.S. Navy photo by Photographer's Mate Airman David J. Hewitt)

22 March 2006, Pacific Ocean – A Japan Maritime Self Defense Force (JMSDF) UH-60J lifts off from the USS Abraham Lincoln (CVN 72) conducting an officer exchange during a passing exercise. (U.S. Navy photo by Photographer's Mate Airman James R. Evans)

16 March 2006, Brassfield-Mora, Iraq – Iraqi Army soldiers on assignment with the U.S. Army 187th Infantry Regiment disembark from a CH-47 Chinook in support of Operation Swarmer. The CH-47 is a twin-engine, tandem rotor helicopter designed for transportation of cargo, troops and weapons during day, night, visual and instrument conditions. (U.S. Navy photo by Photographer's mate 3rd class Shawn Hussong)

23 March 2006, Pacific Ocean – An AV-8B Harrier assigned to the "Tomcats" of VMFA-311 conducts flight operations aboard the amphibious assault ship USS Bonhomme Richard (LHD 6). (U.S. Navy photo by Photographer's Mate Airman Mark Patterson II)

22 March 2006, Pacific Ocean – An F/A-18C Hornet assigned to VFA-151 launches off the USS Abraham Lincoln (CVN 72) during exercises with the Japanese Maritime Self-Defense Force (JMSDF). (U.S. Navy photo by Photographer's Mate Airman Ronald A. Dallatorre)

23 March 2006, Seville, Spain – The first Coast Guard HC-235A medium-range, surveillance, maritime patrol aircraft unveiled at the EADS CASA plant. (U.S. Coast Guard photo courtesy of EADS CASA)

24 March 2006, Al Asad, Iraq – Two CH-46 Sea Knights with the "Wild Goose" of HMM-774 stop at the "hot pits" to get refueled. (U.S. Marine Corps photo by Lance Cpl. Brandon L. Roach)

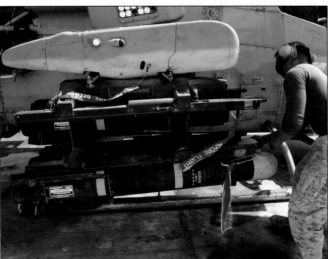

25 March 2006, Al Taqaddum, Iraq – Lance Cpl. Micah E. Vogen puts an AH-1W Super Cobra's M197 20mm automatic gun on safe after the helicopter returns from a mission. (U.S. Marine Corps photo by Cpl. Jonathan K. Teslevich)

25 March 2006, Al Taqaddum, Iraq – Lance Cpl. Micah E. Vogen loads an AGM-114 Hellfire missile aboard an AH-1W Super Cobra. Vogen and the ordnance division Marines with the "Gunfighters" of HMLA-369, Marine Aircraft Group 16 (Reinforced), 3rd Marine Aircraft Wing, are responsible for quickly arming Cobras and UH-1N Hueys before they fly missions. (U.S. Marine Corps photo by Cpl. Jonathan K. Teslevich)

25 March 2006, Al Taqaddum, Iraq – Marines with the ordnance division of the "Gunfighters" of HMLA-369 stand ready to disarm a Bell AH-1W Super Cobra as it settles down on its skids after a mission. (U.S. Marine Corps photo by Cpl. Jonathan K. Teslevich)

24 March 2006, Camp Smedley D. Butler, Okinawa – This GBU-32 Joint Direct Attack Munition (JDAM) will soon be loaded onto an AV-8B Harrier assigned to the "Black Sheep" of VMA-214. (U.S. Marine Corps photo by Lance Cpl. Bryan A Peterson)

03 April 2006, Davis-Monthan AFB, Arizona – Crew members assigned to the "Black Aces" of VFA-41 conduct post flight checks on a F/A-18F Super Hornet during joint Snowbird Operations. (U.S. Air Force photo by Airman 1st Class Veronica Pierce)

13 April 2006, Pensacola, Florida – The last F-14 Tomcat aircraft to fly a combat mission arrives on board Sherman Field. The F-14D (bureau number 161159) was assigned to the "Black Lions" of VF-213 as part of Carrier Air Wing Eight (CVW-8), embarked aboard USS Theodore Roosevelt (CVN 71). The aircraft will become a display aircraft at the National Museum of Naval Aviation. (U.S. Navy photo by Mr. Gary Nichols)

10 April 2006, Sigonella, Sicily – A P-3C Orion anti-submarine aircraft assigned to the "Tridents" of VP-26 prepares for a mission during the squadron's six-month deployment to Sigonella. (U.S. Navy Photo by Photographer's Mate 1st Class John Collins)

13 April 2006, Pacific Ocean – An SH-60B Seahawk assigned to the "Saberhawks" of HSL-47 embarked aboard he aircraft carrier USS Abraham Lincoln (CVN 72) performs a vertical replenishment with the combat stores ship USNS San Jose (T-AFS 7) in the Western Pacific. (U.S. Navy photo by Photographer's Mate Airman Geoffrey Lewis)

13 April 2006, St. Johns, Newfoundland – A Coast Guard C-130 from Air Station Elizabeth City, North Carolina, sits ready for an International Ice Patrol flight around the Arctic Circle. (U.S. Coast Guard photo by PA3 Kip Wadlow)

17 April 2006, Atlantic Ocean – An F/A-18 Super Hornet assigned to the "Jolly Rogers" of VFA-103 prepares to launch from the aircraft carrier USS Dwight D. Eisenhower (CVN 69). (U.S. Navy photo by Chief Photographer's Mate Benjamin D. Olvey)

14 April 2006, Pacific Ocean – Aviation Structural Mechanic 2nd Class Kenneth Poyneer performs routine maintenance on a metal panel from an EA-6B Prowler assigned to the "Lancers" of VAQ-131 in the hangar bay aboard USS Abraham Lincoln (CVN 72). (U.S. Navy photo by Photographer's Mate Airman Geoffrey Lewis)

24 April 2004, Al Asad, Iraq – Sgt. Aaron M. Hefner works on an AH-1W Super Cobra from the "Gunrunners" of HMLA-269 in the setting sun of a warm desert evening. While deployed, the squadron operates as part of MAG-16 (Reinforced). (U.S. Marine Corps photo by Lance Cpl. Brandon L. Roach)

17 April 2006, Atlantic Ocean – An F/A-18F Super Hornet assigned to the "Jolly Rogers" of VFA-103 waits to unfold its wings as an F/A-18E assigned to the world-famous "Pukin' Dogs" of VFA-143 ignites its afterburners aboard the USS Dwight D. Eisenhower (CVN 69). (U.S. Navy photo by Chief Photographer's Mate Benjamin D. Olvey)

18 April 2006, Atlantic Ocean – An E-2C Hawkeye assigned to the "Tigertails" of VAW-125 from Carrier Air Wing Seven (CVW-7) is prepared for launch on the USS Dwight D. Eisenhower (CVN 69) during a Composite Training Unit Exercise. (U.S. Navy photo by Photographer's Mate 3rd Class Christopher B. Long)

25 April 2006, Caribbean Sea – An F/A-18F Super Hornet from the "Red Rippers" of VFA-11 launches from the waist catapult of the USS George Washington (CVN-73) during an air power demonstration. (U.S. Navy photo by Photographer's Mate Airman Apprentice Jennifer Apsey)

17 April 2006, South China Sea – An E-2C Hawkeye, assigned to the "Sun Kings" of VAW-116 conducts aerial maneuvers during an air power demonstration aboard USS Abraham Lincoln (CVN 72). (U.S. Navy photo by Photographer's Mate Airman Ronald A. Dallatorre)

24 April 2006, Al Asad, Iraq – The most prominent feature while looking toward the cockpit of an AH-1W Super Cobra from HMLA-269 is the massive exhausts of the two 2,082-shp General Electric T700 engines. (U.S. Marine Corps photo by Lance Cpl. Brandon L. Roach)

26 April 2006, Atlantic Ocean – A T-45A Goshawk from the "Tigers" of VT-9 catches the arresting wire on the USS Theodore Roosevelt (CVN 71). The Goshawks are embarked aboard the Roosevelt conducting training for new Naval Aviators. (U.S. Navy photo by Photographer's Mate 2nd Class Matthew Bash)

27 April 2006, Persian Gulf – During a passing exercise with the French nuclear-powered aircraft carrier FS Charles de Gaulle (R-91), a Dassault Super-Étendard performed a touch-and-go on the flight deck of the USS Ronald Reagan (CVN 76). (U.S. Navy photo by Photographer's Mate Airman Kathleen Gorby)

25 April 2006, Atlantic Ocean – A C-2A Greyhound assigned to the "Rawhides" of VRC-40 makes an arrested landing on the USS Theodore Roosevelt (CVN 71) during carrier qualifications. (U.S. Navy photo by Photographer's Mate 3rd Class Chris Thamann)

25 April 2006, Atlantic Ocean – A Sailor working on the flight deck brings an aircraft into launch position aboard the USS Theodore Roosevelt (CVN 71). (U.S. Navy photo by Photographer's Mate 3rd Class Chris Thamann)

08 May 2006, Pacific Ocean – Capt. Ryan Colvert from the "Flying Tigers" of HMM-262 (Reinforced) lands his AV-8B Harrier aboard the USS Essex (LHD-2). The 31st Marine Expeditionary Unit and the Sasebo Forward Deployed Amphibious Ready Group are sailing to the Kingdom of Thailand to participate in Exercise Cobra Gold 2006. The pilots of HMM-262 are part of the MEU's air combat element and were conducting carrier qualifications for proficiency training. (U.S. Marine Corps photo by Lance Cpl. Kamran Sadaghiani)

30 April 2006, Atlantic Ocean – Aviation ordnancemen remove a laser guided bomb from an F/A-18C Hornet assigned to the "Rampagers" of VFA-83 aboard the USS Dwight D. Eisenhower. (U.S. Navy Photo by Photographer's Mate Airman Dale Miller)

30 April 2006, Atlantic Ocean – Flight deck personnel prepare a T-45A Goshawk trainer from the "Tigers" of VT-9 before it launches from the USS Theodore Roosevelt (CVN 71). (U.S. Navy photo by Photographer's Mate Airman Stephen A. Early)

10 May 2006, Caribbean Sea – An S-3 Viking assigned to the "Checkmates" of VS-22 refuels another S-3 during routine flight operations from the USS George Washington (CVN 73). Washington was participating in Partnership of the Americas, a maritime training and readiness deployment of the U.S. Naval Forces with Caribbean and Latin American countries in support of the U.S. Southern Command. (U.S. Navy photo by Photographer's Mate 3rd Class Christopher Stephens)

05 May 2006, North Arabian Sea – A French Navy Panther from the FS Charles de Gaulle (R 91) lands aboard the USS Decatur (DDG 73) while providing support to coalition forces in Afghanistan. (U.S. Navy photo by Quartermaster 1st Class David J. Conrad)

10 May 2006, Persian Gulf – Sailors move around the flight deck aboard the USS Ronald Reagan (CVN 76) in preparation for flight operations off the coast of Iraq. (U.S. Navy photo by Photographer's Mate Airman Kathleen Gorby)

11 May 2006, Al Taqaddum, Iraq – An AH-1W Super Cobra manuevers toward the flight line in preparation for a mission over Iraq. The aircraft belongs to the "Vipers" of HMLA-169, Marine Aircraft Group 16 (Reinforced), 3rd Marine Aircraft Wing. (U.S. Marine Corps photo by Cpl. Jonathan K. Teslevich)

11 May 2006, Al Taqaddum, Iraq – Gunnery Sgt. Joseph M. Miley (left) and Cpl. Sean W. Banks work on the environmental system on a AH-1W Super Cobra from the "Vipers" of HMLA-169. (U.S. Marine Corps photo by Cpl. Jonathan K. Teslevich)

19 May 2006, Pacific Ocean – An SH-60B Seahawk assigned to the "Saberhawks" of HSL-47 prepares to land aboard the USS Abraham Lincoln (CVN 72). (U.S. Navy photo by Photographer's Mate Airman James R. Evans)

11 May 2006, Atlantic Ocean – An SH-60F Seahawk assigned to the "Dragonslayers" of HS-11 releases flares while practicing for an air power demonstration aboard the USS Enterprise (CVN 65). (U.S. Navy photo by Photographer's Mate 3rd Class Rob Gaston)

21 May 2006, Arabian Gulf – Sailors assigned to the "Fighting Redcocks" of VFA-22 perform routine maintenance on an F/A-18E Super Hornet aboard the USS Ronald Reagan (CVN 76) while deployed in support of Operations Iraqi Freedom and Enduring Freedom. (U.S. Navy photo by Journalist Seaman Marc Rockwell-Pate)

23 May 2006, Southwest Asia – Aviation Structural Mechanic 3rd Class Brandon Haag hands Aviation Machinist's Mate 2nd Class Nicolas Gardner an engine nacelle while conducting repairs on a P-3C Orion assigned to the "Golden Swordsmen" of VP-47. (U.S. Navy photo by Photographer's Mate 3rd Class Ian W. Anderson)

11 May 2006, Atlantic Ocean – Flight deck Sailors move an E-2C Hawkeye assigned to the "Greyhawks" of VAW-120 on the flight deck of the USS Theodore Roosevelt (CVN 71). (U.S. Navy photo by Photographer's Mate 3rd Class Chris Thamann)

19 May 2006, Pacific Ocean – Forklift operators watch as a SH-60B Seahawk assigned to the "Saberhawks" of HSL-47 lands aboard the USS Abraham Lincoln (CVN 72). (U.S. Navy photo by Photographer's Mate Airman James R. Evans)

27 May 2006, Pacific Ocean – A flight deck Sailor makes preparations to launch an F/A-18E Super Hornet assigned to the "Royal Maces" of VFA-27 off the USS Kitty Hawk (CV 63) during cyclic flight operations. (U.S. Navy photo by Photographer's Mate Airman Stephen W. Rowe)

31 May 2006, Pacific Ocean – The aviation intermediate maintenance department jet shop tests a General Electric F414-GE-400 engine from an F/A-18 Super Hornet on the fantail aboard USS Kitty Hawk (CV 63). (U.S. Navy photo by Photographer's Mate Airman Thomas J. Holt)

02 June 2006, Mediterranean Sea – Boatswain's Mate 2nd Class Damon Box guides an MH-60S Seahawk onto the guided missile frigate USS Simpson (FFG 56) during exercise Phoenix Express. (U.S. Navy photo by Photographer's Mate 2nd Class Herbert D. Banks Jr)

06 June 2006, Jolo, Philippines – Crew members assigned to the "Island Knights" of HSC-25 perform scheduled maintenance during a break from flight quarters aboard the hospital ship USNS Mercy (T-AH 19). (U.S. Navy photo by Chief Photographer's Mate Don Bray)

27 May 2006, New York – A Coast Guard rescue swimmer hangs from a HH-60 Jayhawk helicopter as the crew from Air Station Cape Cod performs a search and rescue demonstration for people enjoying the Fleet Week festivities at the Intrepid Air and Space Museum in New York City. (U.S. Coast Guard photo by PA1 Matthew Belson)

06 June 2006, Pacific Ocean – A CH-46 Sea Knight completes a landing near a V-22 Osprey on the amphibious transport dock USS San Antonio (LPD 17) during compatibility tests. (U.S. Navy photo by Journalist Seaman Recruit Jeff Hall)

07 June 2006, San Diego, California – Master Sgt. Joseph E. Brown (left) and Cpl. Curtis Burton from the "Green Knights" of VMFA-121 load a tactical air launch decoy onto an F/A-18 Hornet at MCAS Miramar. (U.S. Marine Corps photo by Lance Cpl. Scott T. McAdam Jr.)

02 June 2006, Pearl Harbor, Hawaii – The first P-3C Orion assigned to the "Golden Swordsmen" of VP-47 returned home to MCBH Kaneohe Bay from a six month deployment supporting the 5th and 7th fleets. A dozen active patrol squadrons (down from 24 in 1991) operate P-3C AIP and Update III configured aircraft. (U.S. Navy Photo by Photographer's Mate 2nd Class Jennifer L. Bailey)

08 June 2006, Pacific Ocean – A plane director signals to an F/A-18E Super Hornet assigned to the "Eagles" of VFA-115 as it taxies for refueling aboard USS Ronald Reagan (CVN 76). (U.S. Navy photo by Photographer's Mate 3rd Class Kevin S. O'Brien)

09 June 2006, Houston, Texas – The first of four new HH-65C Dolphin helicopters assigned to Coast Guard Air Station Houston overlooks Ellington Field as the morning sun rises. (U.S. Coast Guard photo by PA2 Adam Eggers)

08 June 2006 South China Sea – A BQM-74E aerial target launches from the flight deck of amphibious dock landing ship USS Tortuga (LSD 46) during a missile exercise during the Singapore phase of exercise Cooperation Afloat Readiness and Training (CARAT). The target simulated a threat for the Republic of Singapore Navy ship RSS Vengeance, which took down the drone with a Barak missile. CARAT is an annual series of bilateral maritime training exercises between the U.S. and six Southeast Asia nations designed to build relationships and enhance the operational readiness of the participating forces. (U.S. Navy photo by Mass Communication Specialist 2nd Class John L. Beeman)

08 June 2006 South China Sea – Machinery Repairman 2nd Class Donald Usher removes a JATO unit from a BQM-74E target aboard the amphibious dock landing ship USS Tortuga (LSD 46). (U.S. Navy photo by Mass Communication Specialist 2nd Class John L. Beeman)

08 June 2006, Al Taqaddum, Iraq – Lance Cpl. Dawson K. Hargett (left) hands a CH-46 Sea Knight engine intake to Staff Sgt. Vance Baumer. The Marines are with the "Red Dragons" of HML-268. (U.S. Marine Corps photo by Staff Sgt. Raymie G. Cruz)

08 June 2006, Atlantic Ocean – An F/A-18 Hornet from the "Rough Raiders" of VFA-125 lands aboard the USS Theodore Roosevelt (CVN 71) during routine training off the coast of Virginia. (U.S. Navy photo by Photographer's Mate 3rd Class Jacob Fadley)

11 June 2006, Persian Gulf – A flight deck officer runs along the length of an erected aircraft barricade checking its integrity during a barricade drill on the carrier USS Enterprise (CVN 65). (U.S. Navy photo by Photographer's Mate 2nd Class Milosz Reterski)

10 June 2006, Pacific Ocean – A plane captain signals to the pilot of an E-2C Hawkeye assigned to the "Liberty Bells" of VAW-115 during an engine start-up aboard USS Kitty Hawk (CV 63). Kitty Hawk demonstrates power projection and sea control as the U.S. Navy's only permanently forward-deployed aircraft carrier. (U.S. Navy photo by Photographer's Mate Airman Stephen W. Rowe)

10 June 2006, Arabian Gulf – An F/A-18C Hornet assigned to the "Sidewinders" of VFA-86 launches from the USS Enterprise (CVN 65). Enterprise and embarked Carrier Air Wing One (CVW-1) are currently deployed as part of a routine rotation of U.S. maritime forces in support of Operations Iraqi Freedom and Enduring Freedom (U.S. Navy photo by Photographer's Mate Airman Rob Gaston)

14 June 2006, MCAS Miramar, California – Two Bell Boeing MV-22 Ospreys with Marine Tiltrotor Test and Evaluation Squadron 22 (VMX-22) sit on the flightline after completing a 2,000-mile flight accompanied by two Lockheed KC-130J Hercules aerial refueling aircraft. This was a demonstration of the Osprey's ability to self-deploy over long distances. The Osprey is a multi-engine, dual-piloted, self-deployable, medium lift, vertical takeoff and landing (VTOL) tiltrotor aircraft designed for combat support and Special Operations missions worldwide. It will replace the Corps' aged fleet of CH-46E and CH-53D medium lift helicopters. Much of the exterior of the MV-22 is made of composite materials, making the Osprey one of the military's most unique and technologically advanced aircraft. These aircraft are painted in a unique silver paint scheme that is not representative of operational aircraft, which are low-visibility grey. (U.S. Marine Corps photos by Cpl. Paul Leicht)

12 June 2006, Observation Post Falcons, Iraq – Marines and Navy corpsmen from 3rd Battalion, 5th Marine Regiment, rush a wounded Marine to a CH-46 helicopter for medical evacuation to Camp Taqaddum. Two Marines received concussions in a coordinated insurgent attack. (U.S. Marine Corps photo by Cpl Mark Sixbey)

15 June 2006, Philippine Sea – A Navy ordnanceman stands watch over bombs positioned on the flight deck aboard the USS Kitty Hawk (CV 63) as flight operations are conducted for exercise Valiant Shield 2006. (U.S. Navy photo by Airman Stephen W. Rowe)

15 June 2006, Atlantic Ocean – A student Naval Aviator releases the arresting wire from the tail hook of a T-45C Goshawk after landing aboard the USS Dwight D. Eisenhower (CVN 69). (U.S Navy photo by Photographer's Mate 2nd Class Miguel Angel Contreras)

15 June 2006, Pacific Ocean – An F/A-18C Hornet assigned to the "Blue Diamonds" of VFA-146 comes in for an arrested landing aboard the USS John C. Stennis (CVN 74) during Tailored Ship's Training Availability (TSTA) off the coast of Southern California. (U.S. Navy photo by Airman Alan Willis)

19 June 2006, Yuma, Arizona – Boeing engineers Mark LaVille and Kris Kokkely, mount a Scan Eagle on a pneumatic wedge catapult launcher. Scan Eagle is designed to provide persistent intelligence over a battlefield. (U.S. Marine Corps photo by Cpl. Michael P. Snody)

19 June 2006, Yuma, Arizona – David Hilliard retrieves a Boeing Scan Eagle Unmanned Aerial Vehicle (UAV) from a skyhook that catches the UAV out of mid-air, during training exercise Desert Talon 2-06. (U.S. Marine Corps photo by Sgt Guadalupe M. Deanda III)

18 June 2006, Philippine Sea – U.S. Navy, Air Force, and Marine Corps aircraft fly in formation during the photo portion of Exercise Valiant Shield 2006. The Kitty Hawk Carrier Strike Group is currently participating in Valiant Shield 2006. Valiant Shield focuses on integrated joint training among U.S. military forces, enabling real-world proficiency in sustaining joint forces and in detecting, locating, tracking and engaging units at sea, in the air, on land, and cyberspace in response to a range of mission areas. In addition to Navy and Marine Corps F/A-18 Hornets, the Carrier Strike Group was overflown by Air Force aircraft including a Northrop B-2A Spirit stealth bomber and Boeing F-15 Eagles. (U.S. Navy photo by Photographer's Mate Airman Benjamin Dennis)

18 June 2006, Philippine Sea – An SH-60F Seahawk assigned to HS-14 lifts off from the USS Kitty Hawk (CV 63) during Exercise Valiant Shield 2006, as the USS Ronald Reagan (CVN 76) sails alongside. (U.S. Navy photo by Photographer's Mate Airman Joshua Wayne LeGrand)

18 June 2006, Dhi Qar Province, Iraq – Aviation Ordnanceman 3rd Class Cary Buel installs a MJU-49/B flare into an ALE-47 Counter Measure Dispensing System on a P-3C Orion assigned to VP-9. (U.S. Navy photo by Mass Communication Specialist 1st Class Eric J. Benson)

19 June 2006, Philippine Sea – Airman Janell Kelsey waits to give her signal to launch an F/A-18 from a bow catapult on the USS Ronald Reagan (CVN 76). (U.S. Navy photo by Photographer's Mate Airman Christine Singh)

21 June 2006, Al Taqaddum, Iraq – A Pioneer UAV assigned to Marine Unmanned Aerial Vehicle Squadron Two (VMU-2) on its launch ramp. VMU-2 is deployed in the Al Anbar Province to assist the Iraqi security force. (U.S. Marine Corps photo by Sgt. Jennifer L. Jones)

21 June 2006, Philippine Sea – An SH-60F Seahawk from the "Black Knights" of HS-4 lifts off from the USS Ronald Reagan (CVN 76) during exercise Valiant Shield 2006. (U.S. Navy photo by Photographer's Mate Airman Kathleen Gorby)

21 June 2006, Philippine Sea – An F/A-18C Hornet assigned to the "Dambusters" of VFA-195 conducts a fly-by of the USS Kitty Hawk (CV 63) during Exercise Valiant Shield 2006. (U.S. Navy photo by Photographer's Mate Airman Jimmy C. Pan)

21 June 2006, Pacific Ocean – Sailors signal to a shooter that an F/A-18C Hornet is ready to launch from the USS Kitty Hawk (CV 63) during exercise Valiant Shield 2006. (U.S. Navy photo by Photographer's Mate Airman Benjamin Dennis)

22 June 2006, Philippine Sea – A pilot assigned to the "Fighting Redcocks" of VFA-22 sits in his F/A-18E Super Hornet aboard the USS Ronald Reagan (CVN 76) during Exercise Valiant Shield. (U.S. Navy photo by Photographer's Mate Airman Gary Prill)

23 June 2006, Pacific Ocean – An F/A-18F Super Hornet assigned to the "Death Rattlers" of VFA-154 sits chained to the deck of the USS John C. Stennis (CVN 74) following a day of flight operations. (U.S. Navy photo by Photographer's Mate 3rd Class Philip Morrill)

25 June 2006, Djibouti, Africa – A CH-53E Super Stallion assigned to the "Ironhorses" of HMH-461 sits parked on the flight line at Camp Lemonier while undergoing routine maintenance. In recent years, one of the major thrusts in the helicopter industry has been to produce more aesthetically pleasing designs. One exception to this is the CH-53E and the MH-53E mine countermeasures version, which has regressed significantly with various appurtenances and surfaces at different odd angles. However, beauty is in the eye of the beholder, and the CH-53E can carry more cargo than any other helicopter in the Navy or Marine Corps inventory. (U.S. Navy photo by Photographer's Mate 2nd Class Scott Taylor)

22 June 2006, Philippine Sea – A plane captain directs an F/A-18F Super Hornet during control surface checks prior to takeoff on the USS Abraham Lincoln (CVN 72) during Exercise Valiant Shield 2006. (U.S. Navy photo by Photographer's Mate Airman James R. Evans)

23 June 2006, Pacific Ocean – An aircraft director guides an F/A-18E Super Hornet assigned to the "Royal Maces" of VFA-27 to the No. 2 catapult for launch off the USS Kitty Hawk (CV 63). (U.S. Navy photo by Photographer's Mate Airman Stephen W. Rowe)

23 June 2006, Pacific Ocean – A C-2A Greyhound assigned to the "Providers" of VRC-30 flies over the USS John C. Stennis (CVN 74) off the coast of Southern California. (U.S. Navy photo by Photographer's Mate 3rd Class Philip Morrill)

24 June 2006, Pacific Ocean – An SH-60 Seahawk assigned to the "Golden Falcons" of HS-2 conducts a weapons offload from USS Abraham Lincoln (CVN 72) in the Western Pacific operating area. (U.S. Navy photo by Photographer's Mate Airman Geoffrey Lewis)

23 June 2006, Pacific Ocean – An F/A-18C Hornet assigned to the "Blue Diamonds" of VFA-146 is taxied to launch position on the USS John C. Stennis (CVN 74). Stennis and embarked Carrier Air Wing Nine (CVW-9) are currently underway conducting Tailored Ship's Training Availability (TSTA) off the coast of Southern California. (U.S. Navy photo by Photographer's Mate 3rd Class Philip Morrill)

23 June 2006, Pacific Ocean – Aviation Structural Mechanic (Equipment) 2nd Class Greg Harman conducts a 600-hour periodic maintenance check on an engine in the hangar bay of the USS John C. Stennis (CVN 74). (U.S. Navy photo by Photographer's Mate 1st Class Johnnie Robbins)

02 July 2006, Pacific Ocean – An HH-60H Seahawk assigned to the "Black Knights" of HS-4 fires flares during an air power demonstration above the USS Ronald Reagan (CVN 76). The HH-60H is a variant of the SH-60F designed for combat search and rescue and naval special warfare support. It can operate from aircraft carriers and a variety of other naval and merchant vessels, as well as land bases. The HH-60H retains the same airframe, core avionics, and inherent sea-basing capability of the SH-60F and incorporates many of the ballistic tolerance attributes of the Army UH-60, which are ideally suited for the CSAR mission. The HH-60H's survivability equipment consists of a radar warning system (APR-39(V) 1), a chaff/flare dispenser (ALE-39) and an infrared jammer (ALQ-144(V) 1). (U.S. Navy photo by Mass Communication Specialist Seaman Kathleen Gorby)

29 June 2006, Seville, Spain – First flight of the EADS CN235-300M Maritime Patrol Aircraft (MPA) developed for the Coast Guard Integrated Deepwater System (IDS) Program. (U.S. Coast Guard photo courtesy of Lockheed Martin Corporation)

02 July 2006, Camp Fallujah, Iraq – An AH-1W Super Cobra and CH-46E Sea Knight stand by for casualty evacuation missions. The helicopters are assigned to Marine Aircraft Group 26, 2nd Marine Aircraft Wing. (U.S. Marine Corps photo by Cpl. Ruben D. Maestre)

01 July 2006, Pearl Harbor, Hawaii – A Canadian Royal Navy CF-18 flies off the coast Hawaii in celebration of Canada Day. Eight nations are participating in Rim of the Pacific (RIMPAC) 2006, the world's largest biennial maritime exercise. Conducted in the waters off Hawaii, RIMPAC 2006 brings together military forces from Australia, Canada, Chile, Peru, Japan, the Republic of Korea, the United Kingdom, and the United States. (U.S. Navy photo by Mass Communication Specialist 2nd Class Jason Swink)

01 July 2006, Traverse City, Michigan – The Blue Angels parked on the ramp at Air Station Traverse City. The Navy Flight Demonstration Squadron, the Blue Angels, began its 60th season on 11 March 2006 and are scheduled to perform 69 demonstrations at 36 air show sites throughout the United States, Canada, and the Netherlands. The team is stationed at Forrest Sherman Field, Naval Air Station Pensacola, Florida, during the show season. However, the squadron spends January through March training pilots and new team members at Naval Air Facility El Centro, California. (U.S. Coast Guard photos by Lt. j.g. Jeremy Loeb)

05 July 2006, Al Asad, Iraq – Two F/A-18D Hornets, assigned to the "Knighthawks" of VMFA-533 taxi on their way to a mission over Iraq. VMFA-533 is deployed with 1st Marine Expeditionary Force. Each aircraft is carrying a laser-guided AGM-65E Maverick missile under the wing and a laser designator on the centerline station. The Marines are the only user of the laser-guided variant of the Maverick (most other variants use electro-optical or infrared seekers). (U.S. Marine Corps photo by Lance Cpl. William L. Dubose III)

05 July 2006, Al Asad, Iraq – Two 500-pound laser-guided bombs occupy the station opposite the laser-guided Mavericks on these VMFA-533 Hornets. Laser-guided weapons minimize collateral damage. (U.S. Marine Corps photo by Lance Cpl. William L. Dubose III)

04 July 2006, Pacific Ocean – Fireworks explode over an F/A-18F Super Hornet on the USS Abraham Lincoln (CVN 72) during an Independence Day celebration in Pearl Harbor. (U.S. Navy photo by Mass Communication Specialist Seaman James R. Evans)

03 July 2006, Alaili Dadda, Djibouti – An U.S. Army vehicle clears the landing zone as the dust rises behind one of two Marine Corps CH-53 Super Stallions lifting off from a dry riverbed. U.S. military service members visited Alaili Dadda, a village of 300 near Obok, to assess the difficulty of drilling a well. The long-term goal is to provide running water to several local clinics. (U.S. Navy photo by Mass Communication Specialist 2nd Class Roger S. Duncan)

06 July 2006, Indian Ocean – An F/A-18F Super Hornet, assigned to the "Checkmates" of VFA-211 launches from the USS Enterprise (CVN 65). The Enterprise Carrier Strike Group is currently on a scheduled six-month deployment. (U.S. Navy photo by Mass Communication Specialist 3rd Class N.C. Kaylor)

07 July 2006, Ft. Worth, Texas – The roll-out of the F-35 Joint Strike Fighter (JSF) was held at Lockheed Martin in Ft. Worth, Texas. The Lightning II is expected to replace the AV-8B, A-10, F-16, F/A-18, and United Kingdom Harrier GR.7s and Sea Harriers. (U.S. Navy photo by Chief Mass Communication Specialist Eric A. Clement)

07 July 2006, Pacific Ocean – Aviation boatswains mates clear the arresting wire following the recovery of an F/A-18F Super Hornet from the "Bounty Hunters" of VFA-2 during flight operations aboard *USS Abraham Lincoln (CVN 72)*. (U.S. Navy photo by Mass Communication Specialist Seaman Ronald A. Dallatorre)

11 July 2006, Pacific Ocean – A Sailor assigned to the "Royal Maces" of VFA-27 cleans the canopy of an F/A-18E Super Hornet in preparation for flight operations aboard the conventionally powered aircraft carrier *USS Kitty Hawk (CV 63)*. (U.S. Navy photo by Mass Communication Specialist Seaman Stephen W. Rowe)

08 July 2006, Wheeler Army Airfield, Hawaii – Members of Australia's Clearance Diving Team One board an HH-60H Seahawk from the "Golden Falcons" of HS-2 to train with members of the U.S. Navy's Explosive Ordnance Disposal Group One. (U.S. Navy photo by Mass Communication Specialist 2nd Class Rebecca J. Moat)

11 July 2006, MCAS New River, North Carolina – HML/A-167 crew chief instructor Sergeant Earl M. Day fires the GAU-17 weapon system from a UH-1N Huey. The GAU-17 is a six-barrel Gatling gun that can fire up to 3,000 rounds per minute. (U.S. Marine Corps photo by Lance Cpl. Randall A. Clinton)

13 July 2006, Pacific Ocean – An S-3B Viking assigned to the "Shamrocks" of VS-41 prepares to launch from the USS John C. Stennis (CVN 74). VS-41 will be disestablished with the official ceremony on 27 July 2006, continuing the retirement of the Lockheed anti-submarine aircraft. (U.S. Navy photo by Mass Communication Specialist 1st Class Alan Warner)

12 July 2006, Camp Lemonier, Djibouti – Marines from the 4th Provisional Security Company conduct advanced fast rope training from a CH-53 Super Stallion assigned to HMH-461. (U.S. Navy photo by Mass Communication Specialist 2nd Class Roger S. Duncan)

16 July 2006, Pacific Ocean – E-2C pilots from the "Liberty Bells" of VAW-115 watch cyclic flight operations on board USS Kitty Hawk (CV 63). (U.S. Navy photo by Mass Communication Specialist Seaman Joshua Wayne LeGrand)

13 July 2006, Pacific Ocean – An E-2C Hawkeye assigned to the "Wallbangers" of VAW-117 approaches the USS John C. Stennis (CVN 74) just prior to making an arrested landing. Stennis is currently underway conducting carrier qualifications off the coast of Southern California. (U.S. Navy photo by Mass Communication Specialist 3rd Class Jon Hyde)

16 July 2006, London, England – A Bell V-22 Osprey flies over the River Thames during its arrival to the Farnborough International Air Show. Tens of thousands of people had an opportunity to observe the aircraft for the first time when two Ospreys made the self-deployment from MCAS New River, North Carolina, to Europe. The flight covered more than 4,000 miles, much over it over the North Atlantic Ocean in challenging weather conditions. (U.S. Marine Corps photo courtesy of Bell Helicopters)

17 July 2006, Coronado, California – An S-3B Viking assigned to the "Shamrocks" of VS-41 prepares to land at Naval Air Station Coronado. VS-41 will be disestablished on 27 July 2006. (U.S. Navy photo by Mass Communication Specialist 1st Class Alan Warner)

16 July 2006, Atlantic Ocean – A T-45C Goshawk makes an arrested landing aboard USS George Washington (CVN 73) during carrier qualifications. (U.S. Navy photo by Mass Communication Specialist Seaman Tanner Lange)

17 July 2006, Key West, Florida – Sailors assigned to the "Vampires" of Air Test and Evaluation Squadron Nine (VX-9) prepare an F/A-18 Super Hornet for launch at NAS Key West. (U.S. Navy photo by Mass Communication Specialist 3rd Class Theron J. Godbold)

18 July 2006, Pacific Ocean – Aviation Boatswain's Mate Airman Erin Cruz refuels an AV-8B Harrier assigned to VMA-311, which is part of the reinforcement for HMM-165 aboard the USS Boxer (LHD-4). (U.S. Navy photo by Mass Communication Specialist 3rd Class Noel Danseco)

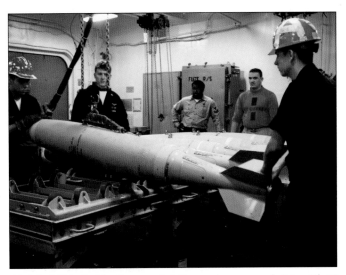

18 July 2006, Pacific Ocean – Aviation ordnancemen hoist a Mk-82 bomb aboard the USS Boxer (LHD 4) while participating in a Composite Training Unit Exercise. (U.S. Navy photo by Mass Communication Specialist Seaman Heather L. Hyatt)

20 July 2006, Pacific Ocean – An F/A-18F Super Hornet assigned to the "Bounty Hunters" of VFA-2 carries Air Force Brig. Gen. Gregory Ihde back to Pearl Harbor after an inspection. (U.S. Navy photo by Mass Communication Specialist Seaman James R. Evans)

22 July 2006, Atlantic Ocean – An F/A-18C Hornet assigned to the "Valions" of VFA-15 is waved off due to a fouled deck on the USS Theodore Roosevelt (CVN 71). (U.S. Navy Photo by Mass Communication Specialist 3rd Class Michael D. Cole)

18 July 2006, Pacific Ocean – An F/A-18F Super Hornet assigned to VFA-2 is signaled on to one of four steam-powered catapults on the flight deck aboard the nuclear-powered aircraft carrier USS Abraham Lincoln (CVN 72). The Lincoln Carrier Strike Group is currently underway in the Hawaiian Operating Area in support of exercise Rim of the Pacific (RIMPAC) 2006. Conducted in the waters off Hawaii, RIMPAC brings together military forces from Australia, Canada, Chile, Peru, Japan, the Republic of Korea, the United Kingdom and the United States. (U.S. Navy Photo by Mass Communication Specialist Seaman Ronald A. Dallatorre)

21 July 2006, Beirut, Lebanon – Marines assigned to the 24th Marine Expeditionary Unit (MEU) assist U.S. citizens onto a CH-46 Sea Knight as they depart the American Embassy in Beirut, Lebanon. At the request of the U.S. Ambassador to Lebanon and at the direction of the Secretary of Defense, the United States Central Command and 24 MEU assisted with the departure of U.S. citizens from Lebanon. (U.S. Marine Corps photo by Cpl. Jeffrey A. Cosola)

20 and 21 July 2006, Suez Canal – The amphibious assault ship USS Iwo Jima (LHD 7) passes under the Mubarak Peace Bridge during its transit through the Suez Canal. Iwo Jima was recently directed to assist in the departure of U.S. citizens from Lebanon. Below, aviation boatswain's mates run across the flight deck to fuel two CH-46 Sea Knights from the "Blue Knights" of HMM-365 for the first trip into Beirut. (U.S. Navy photos by Mass Communication Specialist Seamen Christopher L. Clark and Joshua T. Rodriguez)

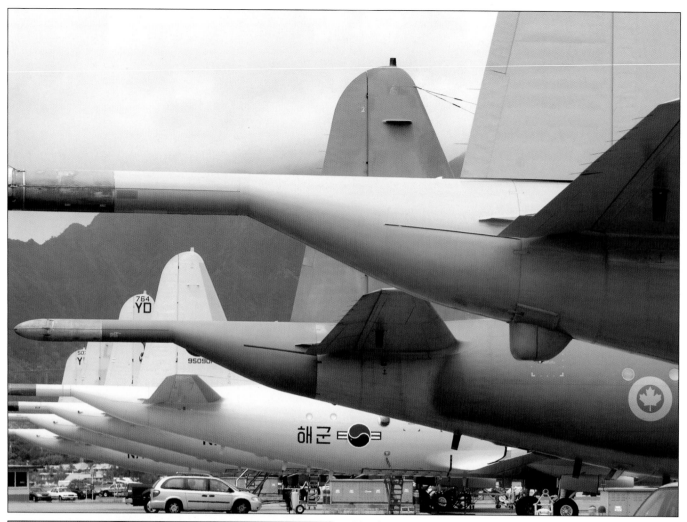

20 July 2006, Kaneohe Marine Corps Base – Canadian and Republic of Korea Navy P-3 Orions are staged on the tarmac in support of Exercise Rim of the Pacific (RIMPAC) 2006. (U.S. Navy photo by Mass Communication Specialist 2nd Class Brandon A. Teeples)

24 July 2006, Pacific Ocean – A CH-53D Sea Stallion lifts off the flight deck of the amphibious assault ship USS Bonhomme Richard (LHD 6) participating in exercise RIMPAC 2006. (U.S. Navy photo by Mass Communication Specialist Seaman Daniel Taylor)

22 July 2006, Atlantic Ocean – An E-2C Hawkeye assigned to the "Bear Aces" of VAW-124 conducts an arrested landing on the USS Theodore Roosevelt (CVN 71), under way maintaining qualifications as part of the Fleet Response Plan. (U.S. Navy photo by Mass Communication Specialist 3rd Class Michael D. Cole)

24 July 2006, Sigonella, Sicily – Aviation Boatswain's Mate (Handling) Airman Tina M. Jones, from NAS Sigonella Fire and Emergency Services Department, is coached through stations of a confidence course by Aviation Boatswains Mate 2nd Class Travis Parsons. The confidence course is a series of activities performed while using a respirator to train personnel to conserve air under stress. (U.S. Navy photo by Mass Communication Specialist 2nd Class Gunnar Gorder)

24 July 2006, Mediterranean Sea – Sailors on the flight deck of the amphibious assault ship USS Iwo Jima (LHD 7) position AV-8B Harriers before the start of the day's flight operations. Iwo Jima is currently part of a large U.S. military mission to assist U.S. citizens in their departure from Lebanon. (U.S Navy photo by Mass Communication Specialist Seaman Christopher L. Clark)

26 July 2006, Seville, Spain – The first CASA CN235-300M on a test flight from the EADS facility in Seville. It is the perfect complement for the Coast Guard fleet of long-range, heavy-lift HC-130 Hercules. (U.S. Coast Guard photo courtesy of EADS CASA)

27 July 2006, Atlantic Ocean – An EA-6B Prowler assigned to the "Shadowhawks" of VAQ-141 prepares for an arrested landing on the USS Theodore Roosevelt (CVN 71). (U.S. Navy photo by Mass Communication Specialist 3rd Class Randall Damm)

27 July 2006, Coronado, California – S-3B Viking aircraft surround the disestablishment ceremony for the "Shamrocks" of Sea Control Squadron Forty One (VS-41) held at Naval Air Station North Island. VS-41 is being disestablished after 46 years distinguished service. (U.S. Navy photo by Mass Communication Specialist Seaman Damien E. Horvath)

27 July 2006, Atlantic Ocean – An F-14D Tomcat assigned to the "Tomcatters" of VF-31 sits on the USS Theodore Roosevelt (CVN 71) while underway as part of the Fleet Response Plan. (U.S. Navy photo by Mass Communication Specialist 3rd Class Randall Damm)

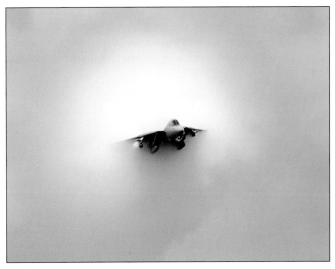

28 July 2006, Atlantic Ocean – An F-14D Tomcat assigned to the "Tomcatters" of VF-31 makes a near supersonic fly-by of the USS Theodore Roosevelt (CVN 71). (U.S. Navy Photo by Mass Communications Specialist 3rd Class Nathan Laird)

28 July 2006, Atlantic Ocean – An F-14D Tomcat assigned to the "Tomcatters" of VF-31 maneuvers over the number three catapult aboard USS Theodore Roosevelt (CVN 71). This was the last launch of an F-14 from an aircraft carrier, marking the end of an era for Naval Aviation. The F-14 will officially retire in September 2006, after 32 years of service to the fleet. (U.S. Navy photos by Mass Communications Specialist Seaman Sheldon Rowley and Mass Communications Specialist 3rd Class Nathan Laird)

U.S. Naval Aviation

02 August 2006, Pacific Ocean – An SH-60B Seahawk from the "Scorpions" of HSL-49 hovers alongside the guided-missile destroyer USS Howard (DDG 83). (U.S. Navy photo by Mass Communication Specialist Seaman Apprentice Joshua Valcarcel)

30 July 2006, Pacific Ocean – An F/A-18F assigned to the "Bounty Hunters" of VFA-2 performs during an air power demonstration over the USS Abraham Lincoln (CVN 72). (U.S. Navy photo by Mass Communication Specialist 3rd Class M. Jeremie Yoder)

02 August 2006, Patuxent River, Maryland – A single-seat F/A-18E is being used by the Naval Air Test Center's Strike Test Directorate to verify aspects of the performance of the new EA-18G Growler. (U.S. Navy photo)

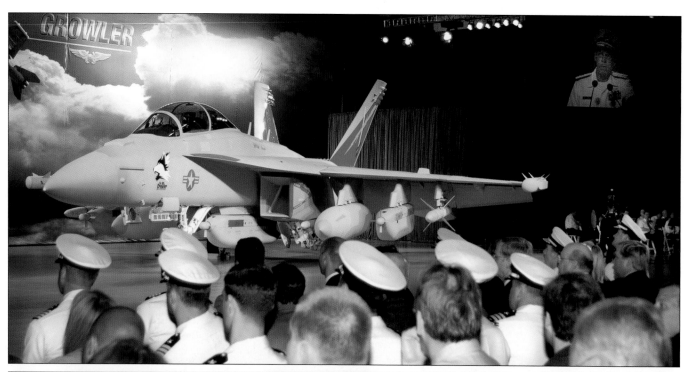

03 August 2006, St. Louis, Missouri – Chief of Naval Operations Adm. Mike Mullen speaks during the EA-18G Growler roll-out ceremony held at The Boeing Company facility in St. Louis. The EA-18G Growler is being developed to replace the fleet's current carrier-based EA-6B Prowler. The next-generation electronic attack aircraft, for the U.S. Navy, combines the combat-proven F/A-18 Super Hornet with a state-of-the-art electronic warfare avionics suite. The EA-18G will feature an airborne electronic attack suite based on Northrop Grumman's Improved Capability III system, a radically new jamming and information warfare system. The EA-18G is expected to enter initial operational capability in 2009. (U.S. Air Force photo by Mr. Marv Lynchard)

04 August 2006, Al Asad, Iraq – Cpl. Dustin M. Hawkins guides an AV-8B Harrier, piloted by his cousin, Lt. Col. James D. Hawkins. James, the executive officer of Marine Aircraft Group 16 (Reinforced), 3rd Marine Aircraft Wing, occasionally gets the chance to fly for his cousin's squadron, Marine Attack Squadron 513, MAG-16, 3rd MAW, allowing them time to catch up with one another. (U.S. Marine Corps photo by Lance Cpl. Brian J. Holloran)

04 August 2006, Astoria, Oregon – Forty-two Sikorsky HH-60J Jayhawks are operated by the Coast Guard. With its twin T700-GE-401C engines, the Jayhawk can fly up to 300 miles offshore, remain on scene 45 minutes, hoist six people on board, and return to its point of origin with a safe fuel reserve. The HH-60J will fly comfortably at 140 knots for six to seven hours. Though normally stationed ashore, the Jayhawk can be carried aboard 270-foot WMEC and 378-foot WHEC Coast Guard cutters. (U.S. Coast Guard photo PA2 Sarah Foster-Snell)

07 August 2006, Indian Ocean – An F/A-18E Super Hornet from the "Royal Maces" of VFA-27 launches from the No. 3 waist catapult while an EA-6B Prowler from the "Gauntlets" of VAQ-136 maneuvers over the No. 2 catapult in preparation for launch aboard USS Kitty Hawk (CV 63). Kitty Hawk typically conducts flight operations over a 12-hour period each day, including both day and night missions. (U.S. Navy photo by Mass Communication Specialist Seaman Stephen W. Rowe)

08 August 2006, Maura, Brunei Darussalam – Lt. Cmdr. John Wigglesworth discusses the features of a VP-69 P-3C Orion with Royal Brunei Air Force Capt. Dzulkiflee Shamsol. (U.S. Navy photo by Mass Communication Specialist 1st Class Kathryn Whittenberger)

08 August 2006, South China Sea – A C-2A Greyhound assigned to the "Providers" of VRC-30 landing aboard USS Kitty Hawk (CV 63). The C-2A is a carrier on-board delivery (COD) aircraft. (U.S. Navy photo by Mass Communication Specialist Seaman Joshua Wayne LeGrand)

15 August 2006, Indian Ocean – An F/A-18C Hornet assigned to the "Golden Dragons" of VFA-192 launches from the USS Kitty Hawk (CV 63) during flight operations. (U.S. Navy photo by Mass Communication Specialist Seaman Stephen W. Rowe)

17 August 2006, Pacific Ocean – Combat Cargo personnel prepare to assist with offloading wounded Marines during a mass casualty drill on the amphibious assault ship USS Boxer (LHD 4). (U.S. Navy photo Mass Communication Specialist 1st Class S. H. Vanderwerff)

17 August 2006, Atlantic Ocean – Personnel aboard the USS George Washington (CVN 73) connect a cable to an HSC-28 MH-60S to transfer ammunition to the USNS Mount Baker (T-AE 34). (U.S. Navy photo by Mass Communication Specialist Seaman Ian Schoeneberg)

18 August 2006, Pacific Ocean – A holdback bar operator sprints from the front of an E-2C Hawkeye assigned to VAW-113 as it prepares to launch from the USS Ronald Reagan. (U.S. Navy photo by Mass Communication Specialist 3rd Class Marc Rockwell-Pate)

19 August 2006, Pacific Ocean – AV-8B Harriers from the "Black Knights" of HMM-264 (Reinforced), 26th Marine Expeditionary Unit, practice take-offs from the flight deck of the USS Bataan (LHD 5). (U.S. Marine Corps photo by Lance Cpl. Jeremy T. Ross)

21 August 2006, Indian Ocean – An S-3B Viking assigned to the "Maulers" of VS-32 makes an arrested landing on the USS Enterprise (CVN 65).
(U.S. Navy photo by Mass Communication Specialist Seaman Michael Banzhaf)

23 August 2006, Al Asad, Iraq – A Marine with MWSS-274 waits to complete fueling an F/A-18D Hornet. The mission of the mobile refuelers section is to conduct cold tactical aircraft refueling to all squadrons, including coalition and multi-national aircraft at Al Asad Air Base. (U.S. Marine Corps photo by Cpl. Jonathan K. Teslevich)

23 August 2006, Sigonella, Sicily – Aviation Ordnanceman 3rd Class Giancarlo Rosasarias of Los Angeles, directs a P-3C Orion assigned to the "War Eagles" of VP-16 to a parking area after a training flight over the Mediterranean. (U.S. Navy photo by Mass Communication Specialist Third Class Charles E. White)

30 August 2006, Chicago, Illinois – The stars and director of the Coast Guard-themed film "The Guardian" experienced a ride on Station Caulmet Harbor's 25-foot small boat while an HH-65 looks on. (U.S. Coast Guard photo by PA3 Bill Colclough)

30 August 2006, Dili, Timor Leste – An Australian Army HH-60 Blackhawk helicopter from B Squadron, 5th Aviation Regiment, lands aboard the hospital ship USNS Mercy (T-AH 19). (U.S. Navy photo by Mass Communication Specialist 2nd Class Erika N. Jones)

23 August 2006, Atlantic Ocean – A Scan Eagle Unmanned Aerial Vehicle (UAV) launches from a pneumatic wedge catapult launcher aboard the USS Saipan (LHA 2). (U.S. Navy photo by Mass Communication Specialist Seaman Patrick W. Mullen III)

25 August 2006, Pensacola Bay – A TH-57 from HT-8 at NAS Whiting Field, makes a landing aboard the Navy Helicopter Landing Trainer (HLT) IX-514, marking the 100,000th consecutive accident-free landing on the vessel. (U.S. Navy photo by Gary Nichols)

28 August 2006, Pearl Harbor, Hawaii – Outrider 50, also known as "Kekaha Town" lands at Ford Island to become part of the Pacific Air Museum. The UH-3H Sea King is one of three aircraft being decommissioned from the Pacific Missile Range Facility on Kuaui, capping off a nearly 40-year career during which it logged more than 13,500 flight hours. (U.S. Navy photo by Mass Communication Specialist Joe Kane)

26 August 2006, Indian Ocean – An MH-60S from the "Island Knights" of HCS-25 carries cargo from the combat stores ship USNS Concord (T-AFS 5) to the USS Kitty Hawk (CV 63). (U.S. Navy photo by Mass Communication Specialist Seaman Joshua Wayne LeGrand)

30 August 2006, Pacific Ocean – An F/A-18C Hornet assigned to the "Sunliners" of VFA-81 lands on the USS Nimitz (CVN 68), during routine flight operations off the coast of Southern California. (U.S. Navy photo by Mass Communication Specialist Seaman Jake Berenguer)

02 September 2006, Al Asad, Iraq – An F/A-18 Hornet from the "Flying Gators" of VMFA-142 prepares for take off for a ferry flight back to its home base at Naval Air Station Atlanta, Georgia. The Hornet was one of the last aircraft from the squadron to leave Iraq after a seven-month deployment in support of Operation Iraqi Freedom. (U.S. Marine Corps photo by Lance Cpl. James D. Hamel)

31 August 2006, Al Taqaddum, Iraq – Cpl. Miles P. Wilson fires a 0.50-caliber machine gun from a CH-46 Sea Knight during a test flight with the "Purple Foxes" of HMM-364. (U.S. Marine Corps photo by Cpl. Jonathan K. Teslevich)

31 August 2006, Al Taqaddum, Iraq – A CH-46 Sea Knight helicopter spins its rotors in HMM-364's working space just before a casualty evacuation mission in central Iraq, approximately 45 miles west of Baghdad. (U.S. Marine Corps photo by Cpl. Jonathan K. Teslevich)

06 September 2006, Arabian Sea – Aviation Boatswain's Mate Airman Andres Rivera directs a C-2A Greyhound assigned to the "Rawhides" of VRC-40 into position for launch on the USS Enterprise (CVN 65). Enterprise Carrier Strike Group and embarked Carrier Air Wing One (CVW-1) are currently on a scheduled six-month deployment in Southwest Asia. Many parts of the C-2A, including the engines and basic wing structure, are shared with the E-2C Hawkeye. (U.S. Navy photo by Mass Communication Specialist Seaman Brandon Morris)

07 September 2006, Atlantic Ocean – An MH-60S Seahawk, assigned to the "Dragon Whalers" of HSC-28 transfers ordnance from the fast combat support ship USNS Arctic (T-AOE 8) to the USS Dwight D. Eisenhower (CVN 69). (U.S. Navy photo by Mass Communication Specialist 2nd Class Miguel Angel Contreras)

07 September 2006, Key West, Florida – Director of Business Development Peter Bale readies an Aerosonde unmanned aerial vehicle (UAV) for a flight. The UAV is designed to gather near-surface data on hurricanes as they threaten coastline areas. (U.S. Navy photo by Mass Communication Specialist 2nd Class Timothy Cox)

07 September 2006, San Diego, California – Chiefs and chief selectees from the San Diego area stand in formation during colors for Chief Petty Officers (CPO) Day aboard the San Diego Aircraft Carrier Museum, Ex-USS Midway. CPO Day consisted of guest speakers, marching in Balboa Park, and community service projects through out the San Diego area. (U.S. Navy photo by Mass Communication Specialist Seaman Jonathan Husman)

08 September 2006, East China Sea – An MH-60S crewman from HCS-25 gives hand signals to an aircraft director during a vertical replenishment between USS Kitty Hawk (CV 63) and the combat stores ship USNS Concord (T-AFS 5). (U.S. Navy photo by Mass Communication Specialist Seaman Joshua Wayne LeGrand)

09 September 2006, Arabian Sea – An MH-60S Seahawk, assigned to the "Bay Raiders" of HSC-28, transfers supplies from the fast combat support ship USNS Supply (T-AOE 6) to the USS Enterprise (CVN 65). (U.S. Navy photo by Mass Communication Specialist Second Class Stacee Fitzgerald)

09 September 2006, Virginia Beach, Virginia – F/A-18F Super Hornets, F-14 Tomcats, and F/A-18C Hornets fly in formation during the Fleet Air Power Demonstration at the 2006 Naval Air Station Oceana Air Show. (U.S. Navy photo by Mass Communication Specialist 3rd Class Brandon E. Holmes)

09 September 2006, Virginia Beach, Virginia – Two F-14 Tomcats take off during the 2006 Naval Air Station Oceana air show. The 2006 NAS Oceana Air Show was themed "Salute to the Blue Angels; 60 Years of Aerial Excellence." (U.S. Navy photo by Mass Communication Specialist 3rd Class Brandon E. Holmes)

09 September 2006, Arabian Sea – Aviation ordnanceman study training materials while standing watch over racks of GBU-38 Joint Attack Direct Munitions (JDAM) on the hangar deck aboard the USS Enterprise (CVN 65). Enterprise and embarked Carrier Air Wing One (CVW-1) are currently underway on a scheduled six-month deployment. For the last five consecutive days aircraft assigned to CVW-1 have provided support to International Security Assistance Force (ISAF) troops on the ground as part of Operations Medusa and Enduring Freedom near Kandahar, Afghanistan. Coordinated with coalition air forces and ISAF troops on the ground, Enterprise aircraft provided close air support for ISAF troops encountering resistance from Taliban extremists in multiple locations around Kandahar on 6 and 7 September 2006. (U.S. Navy photograph by Mass Communication Specialist Seaman Devonte Jones)

12 September 2006, Atlantic Ocean – E-2C Hawkeyes and C-2A Greyhounds from the "Greyhawks" of VAW-120 and an F/A-18C Hornet from Test Squadron Twenty Three (VX-23) prepare to launch from the USS Dwight D. Eisenhower (CVN 69) during carrier qualifications. (U.S. Navy photo by Mass Communication Specialist 2nd Class Miguel Angel Contreras)

11 September 2006, Atlantic Ocean – Plane captains assigned to the "Greyhawks" of VAW-120 carry tiedown chains while awaiting the launch of a C-2A Greyhound aboard the USS Dwight D. Eisenhower (CVN 69). (U.S. Navy photo by Mass Communication Specialist 3rd Class Jonathon Rownd)

12 September 2006, over Jacksonville, Florida – A pair of T-45 Goshawks from Training Air Wing Two (TRAWING-2) at NAS Kingsville, Texas, make their way to the Nimitz-class aircraft carrier USS Theodore Roosevelt (CVN 71). Twenty-Four student aviators will complete their carrier qualifications aboard Roosevelt. (U.S. Navy photo by Lt. j.g. Lee Thackston)

12 September 2006, NAS Cecil Field, Florida – Lt. j.g. Dylan Schoo from VT-21 at NAS Kingsville, Texas, prepares to take-off in his T-45 Goshawk at Cecil Field. Schoo was one of 24 student aviators from TRAWING-2 to make their first arrested landing on an aircraft carrier and complete their carrier qualifications aboard USS Theodore Roosevelt (CVN 71). (U.S. Navy photo by Lt. j.g. Lee Thackston)

13 September 2006, Pacific Ocean – F/A-18C Hornets assigned to the "Lancers" of VFMA-212 fly next to a KC-130 assigned to the "Sumos" of VMGR-152 during an aerial refueling mission as part of Exercise Southern Frontier. (U.S. Marine Corps photo by Sgt. David J. Hercher)

12 September 2006, Atlantic Ocean – E-2C Hawkeyes assigned to the "Greyhawks" of VAW-120 are tied down to the flight deck prior to carrier qualifications starting for the day aboard the USS Dwight D. Eisenhower (CVN 69). (U. S. Navy photo by Mass Communication Specialist 2nd Class Miguel Angel Contreras)

12 September 2006, Pacific Ocean – Sailors aboard the USS Kitty Hawk (CV 63) get an F/A-18F Super Hornet assigned to VFA-102 into position for launch during a squadron fly-off. The F-model is a combat-capable two-seat version of the F/A-18E. (U.S. Navy photo by Mass Communication Specialist Seaman Joshua Wayne LeGrand)

15 September 2006, China Lake, California – An F/A-18F Super Hornet equipped with an APG-79 AESA radar, conducts an operational test mission to evaluate the radar's ability to support the Strike Coordination and Reconnaissance mission. The Super Hornet used the AESA's radar mapping modes to detect and target "enemy" vehicles on the vast bombing ranges of Naval Air Weapons Station (NAWS) China Lake. (U.S. Navy photo by Cmdr. Ian Anderson)

13 September 2006, Arabian Sea – Aviation Ordnanceman 3rd Class Tristan Rose inspects ordnance staged at the bomb farm on the flight deck of the USS Enterprise (CVN 65). (U.S. Navy photo by Mass Communication Specialist 2nd Class Milosz Reterski)

17 September 2006, Yokosuka, Japan – An E-2C Hawkeye assigned to the "Liberty Bells" of VAW-115 performs a fly-over for Sailors and their families on the USS Kitty Hawk (CV 63) during a family day cruise. More than 2,200 family members and guests embarked aboard Kitty Hawk for the cruise, which included an air power demonstration, shipboard tours, and ship maneuvers by three warships of the Kitty Hawk Carrier Strike Group. (U.S. Navy photo by Mass Communication Specialist Seaman Stephen W. Rowe)

14 September 2006, Atlantic Ocean – A C-2A Greyhound assigned to the "Rawhides" of VRC-40 prepares to launch from the USS Dwight D. Eisenhower (CVN 69). (U.S. Navy photo by Mass Communication Specialist Seaman Dale Miller)

18 September 2006, Atlantic City, New Jersey – Coast Guard rescue swimmers from Coast Guard Air Station Atlantic City train off of the coast using an HH-65 Dolphin. (U.S. Coast Guard photo by PAC Tom Sperduto)

22 September 2006, Jacksonville, Florida – Lt. j.g. Dylan Schoo assigned to the "Red Hawks" of VT-21 at NAS Kingsville, Texas, performs a pre-flight inspection of his T-45 Goshawk on the flight line at Cecil Field. (U.S. Navy photo by Lt. j.g. Lee Thackston)

22 September 2006, Virginia Beach, Virginia – An F-14D Tomcat assigned to the "Tomcatters" of VF-31 prepares for its final take-off during the "Sunset Ceremony" held at NAS Oceana. (U.S. Navy photo by Mass Communication Specialist 3rd Class Jason R. Zalasky)

22 September 2006, San Diego, California – A U.S. Air Force CV-22 Osprey prepares for an exhibition and training exercise with U.S. Navy SEALS at NAS North Island. (U.S. Navy photo by Mass Communication Specialist Seaman Daniel A. Barker)

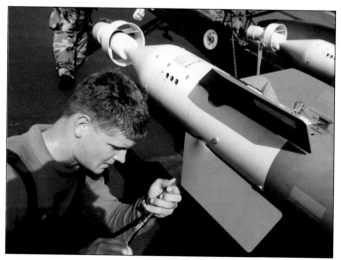

22 September 2006, Arabian Sea – Aviation Ordnanceman 3rd Class Mark Kirchner installs fins on a GBU-12 laser-guided bomb aboard the USS Enterprise (CVN 65). (U.S. Navy photograph by Mass Communication Specialist 2nd Class Milosz Reterski)

22 September 2006, Atlantic Ocean – A T-45 Goshawk trainer prepares to make an arrested landing aboard USS Theodore Roosevelt (CVN 71). (U.S. Navy photo by Mass Communication Specialist 3rd Class Randall Damm)

27 September 2006, Washington, D.C. – The Coast Guard began flying its HH-65C Dolphins out of National Airport, assuming low-altitude aviation interception operations for the North American Aerospace Defense Command. (U.S. Coast Guard photo)

23 September 2006, Arabian Sea – Team members of Explosive Ordnance Disposal Mobile Unit Six (EODMU-6), Detachment 14, are suspended from an HH-60H Seahawk, attached to the "Dragonslayers" of HS-11 during a Special Purpose Insertion and Extraction (SPIE) training exercise aboard the USS Enterprise (CVN 65). SPIE is a method to rapidly insert or extract Special Forces from terrain not suitable for helicopter landings. (U.S. Navy photos by Mass Communication Specialist 2nd Class Milosz Reterski and Mass Communication Specialist Seaman Rob Gaston)

27 September 2006, Al Anbar Province, Iraq – Marine landing support specialists with Helicopter Support Team, Combat Logistics Battalion 1, Combat Logistics Regiment 1, 1st Marine Logistics Group (Forward), await a CH-53 Super Stallion to lift a damaged HH-60 Blackhawk. The team's primary mission is to lead planes down the runway and ensure they make it to their destination, but while on recovery operations, they have successfully rescued four helicopters since arriving here spring 2006. (U.S. Marine Corps photo by Cpl. James B. Hoke)

28 September 2006, MCAS New River, North Carolina – This early-production MV-22 Osprey assigned to the "Raptors" of VMMT-204 is no longer used in operations; instead, it is used as a ground maintenance trainer. (U.S. Marine Corps photo by Lance Cpl. Randall A. Clinton)

28 September 2006, MCAS New River, North Carolina – An MV-22 Osprey flies over the VMMT-204 flightline. Marines transitioning from the CH-46E to the new MV-22 go through VMMT-204 for training before joining an operational squadron. (U.S. Marine Corps photo by Lance Cpl. Randall A. Clinton)

02 October 2006, Persian Gulf – Marines assigned to the 24th Marine Expeditionary Unit (Special Operations Capable) board a CH-53E Sea Stallion on the flight deck of the amphibious assault ship USS Iwo Jima (LHD 7). (U.S. Navy photo by Mass Communication Specialist Seaman Joshua T. Rodriguez)

05 October 2006, Pacific Ocean – An AV-8B Harrier assigned to the "Blacksheep" of VMA-214 launches from the amphibious assault ship USS Bonhomme Richard (LHD 6) The launch took place during Bonhomme Richard's transit to San Francisco to take part in Fleet Week 2006 festivities. (U.S. Navy Photo by Mr. John F. Williams)

07 October 2006, San Francisco, California – An F/A-18 Hornet makes an approach to the USS Nimitz (CVN 68) for a touch-and-go while in the San Francisco Bay as part of the Fleet Week 2006 activities. (U.S. Coast Guard photo by Petty Officer 3rd Class Kevin J. Neff)

12 October 2006, The Republic of the Philippines – An airfield management specialist with the Philippine Air Force salutes the pilot of an F/A-18C Hornet assigned to the "Crusaders" of VMFA-122 at Clark Air Base. (U.S. Marine Corps photo by Lance Cpl. David Rogers)

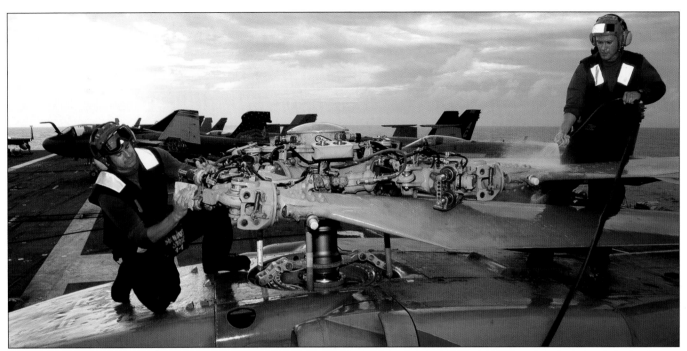

07 October 2006, Atlantic Ocean – Aviation Machinist's Mate Airman Damian Gomez and Airman Robert Aidrete assigned to the "Nightdippers" of HS-5 conduct an anti-corrosion wash down on an SH-60F Seahawk aboard the USS Dwight D. Eisenhower (CVN 69). (U.S. Navy photo by Mass Communication Specialist 2nd Class Miguel Angel Contreras)

13 October 2006, Arabian Sea – A pilot of an EA-6B Prowler attached to the "Rooks" of VAQ-137 performs preflight checks prior to launch from the USS Enterprise (CVN 65). (U.S. Navy photo by Mass Communication Specialist Seaman Brandon Morris)

13 October 2006, Pacific Ocean – An F/A-18F Super Hornet assigned to the "Black Aces" of VFA-41 launches from the USS Nimitz (CVN 68) off the coast of Southern California. (U.S. Navy photo by Mass Communication Specialist 3rd Class Roland Franklin)

14 October 2006, San Diego, California – The U.S. Navy Blue Angels' F/A-18 Hornets grace the runway on Marine Corps Air Station Miramar as they bring their demonstration to a close during the 2006 Miramar Air Show. (U.S. Marine Corps photo by Lance Cpl. Kelly R. Chase)

14 October 2006, MCAS Miramar, California – An AH-1W Super Cobra watches as two CH-46 Sea Knights land on the flight line during a demonstration at the 50th annual Miramar air show. (U.S. Marine Corps photo by Lance Cpl. Kelly R. Chase)

15 October 2006, Arabian Sea – An F/A-18C assigned to the "Knighthawks" of VFA-136 tests its flare countermeasure system before heading into Afghanistan on a close air support mission from the USS Enterprise (CVN 65). (U.S. Navy by Lt. Peter Scheu)

15 October 2006, South China Sea – Marines assigned to the "Tomcats" of VMA-311 load a GBU-38 Joint Attack Direct Munition onto an AV-8B Harrier during a synchronization test. (U.S. Navy photo by Mass Communication Specialist Marvin E. Thompson Jr.)

19 October 2006, Atlantic Ocean – A C-2A Greyhound assigned to the "Rawhides" of VRC-40 makes an arrested landing aboard USS Theodore Roosevelt (CVN 71). (U.S. Navy photo by Mass Communication Specialist 3rd Class Nathan Laird)

15 October 2006, Afghanistan – A Navy F/A-18C Hornet from the "Knighthawks" of VFA-136 receives fuel from an Air Force KC-10 Extender during a close air support mission over Afghanistan. (U.S. Navy photo by Lt. Peter Scheu)

23 October 2006, Mediterranean Sea – Aviation Ordnanceman Airman Harold Doe assigned to the "Wildcats" of VFA-131 tightens a bolt on a laser-guided practice bomb on an F/A-18 Hornet aboard the USS Dwight D. Eisenhower (CVN 69). (U.S. Navy photo by Mass Communication Specialist 2nd Class Miguel Angel Contreras)

23 October 2006, Mediterranean Sea – Lt. Kimball Terres, a "shooter" aboard the USS Dwight D. Eisenhower (CVN 69), checks the flight deck's crosswind gages before launching an EA-6B Prowler assigned to the "Patriots" of VAQ-140. (U.S. Navy photo by Mass Communication Specialist 2nd Class Miguel Angel Contreras)

17 October 2006, Pacific Ocean – Flight deck personnel prepare a T-45A Goshawk from the "Eagles" of VT-7 to taxi across the flight deck aboard the USS Ronald Reagan (CVN 76) during carrier qualifications off the coast of Southern California. (U.S. Navy photo by Mass Communication Specialist 2nd Class Aaron Burden)

25 October 2006, Al Taqaddum, Iraq – A UH-1N Huey sits buttoned up on the flight line during a light rain. The helicopter belongs to the "Scarface" of HMLA-367, Marine Aircraft Group 16 (Reinforced), 3rd Marine Aircraft Wing (Forward). (U.S. Marine Corps photo by Cpl. Jonathan K. Teslevich)

07 November 2006, Atlantic Ocean – An AV-8B Harrier assigned to the "Black Knights" of HMM-264 launches from the flight deck of amphibious assault ship USS Bataan (LHD 5). The Bataan Expeditionary Strike Group is conducting a Composite Training Unit Exercise (COMPTUEX) with the 26th Marine Expeditionary Unit. (U.S. Navy photo by Mass Communication Specialist 3rd Class Jeremy L. Grisham)

02 November 2006, Red Sea – An F/A-18 Hornet assigned to the "Wildcats" of VFA-131 launches off a waist catapult aboard USS the Dwight D. Eisenhower (CVN 69) while another F/A-18 awaits its turn. (U.S. Navy photo by Mass Communication Specialist Seaman Clarence McCloud)

03 November 2006, Hadithah Al Anbar, Iraq – Marines from Fox Company, 2nd Platoon, 3rd Squad secure the site of an unmanned aerial vehicle that crash landed on the roof of a house in the city of Hadithah while recovery issues are organized. (U.S. Marine Corps photo by Sgt. Jason L. Jensen)

09 November 2006, Arabian Sea – An E-2C Hawkeye assigned to the "Tigertails" of VAW-125 launches from the USS Dwight D. Eisenhower (CVN 69). Eisenhower and embarked Carrier Air Wing Seven (CVW-7) are currently on a scheduled deployment in support of Maritime Security Operations. (U.S. Navy photo by Mass Communication Specialist 2nd Class Miguel Angel Contreras)

05 November 2006, Pacific Ocean – An F/A-18F Super Hornet assigned to the "Diamondbacks" of VFA-102 completes a high-speed flyby as part of an air power demonstration for visitors aboard USS Kitty Hawk (CV 63). (U.S. Navy photo by Mass Communication Specialist 3rd Class Jarod Hodge)

07 November 2006, Atlantic Ocean – Marines assigned to the 26th Marine Expeditionary Unit board a CH-46 helicopter assigned to the "Black Knights" of HMM-264 (Reinforced) aboard the amphibious assault ship USS Bataan (LHD 5). (U.S. Navy photo by Mass Communication Specialist 2nd Class Tommy E. Lamkin Jr.)

14 November 2006, Pacific Ocean – An F/A-18C Hornet assigned to the "Argonauts" of VFA-147 launches from the USS John C. Stennis (CVN 74). Serving as the flagship for Commander, Carrier Strike Group Three (CSG-3), Stennis is currently participating in a Joint Task Force Exercise, the third at-sea phase of the Strike Group's pre-deployment training cycle. (U.S. Navy Photo by Mass Communication Specialist 3rd Class Ron Reeves)

12 November 2006, Pacific Ocean – An SH-60B Seahawk helicopter from the "Warlords" of HSL-51 sits on the deck of the Japanese Maritime Self-Defense Force destroyer JDS Kurama (DDH 144) as JDS Samidare (DD 106) sails behind during exercise ANNUALEX. (U.S. Navy photo by Aviation Warfare Systems Operator 2nd Class Jacob Gonzales)

U.S. Naval Aviation

14 November 2006, Pacific Ocean – An F/A-18C Hornet from the "Argonauts" of VFA-147 launches off the USS John C. Stennis (CVN 74). The Hornet uses its afterburners during launch. (U.S. Navy photo by Mass Communication Specialist 3rd Class Ron Reeves)

14 November 2006, Portsmouth, Virginia – Sailors assigned to the air department aboard the USS Harry S. Truman (CVN 75) raise the aircraft barricade during a training drill in preparation for upcoming sea trials. Truman is conducting a docked planned incremental availability (PIA) at the Norfolk Naval Shipyard,. (U.S. Navy photo by Mass Communications Specialist Seaman Justin Lee Losack)

14 November 2006, China Lake, California – A Micro Air Vehicle (MAV) flies over a simulated combat area during an operational test flight. The MAV is in the operational test phase with military explosive ordnance disposal (EOD) teams to evaluate its short-range reconnaissance capabilities. (U.S. Navy photo by Mass Communication Specialist 3rd Class Kenneth G. Takada)

14 November 2006, Pacific Ocean – Sailors assigned to the "Dambusters" of VFA-195 wipe down an F/A-18 Hornet aboard USS Kitty Hawk (CV 63). The Kitty Hawk Carrier Strike Group was conducting an exercise with 90 ships from the Japanese Maritime Self-Defense Force. (U.S. Navy photo by Mass Communication Specialist 3rd Class Jarod Hodge)

18 November 2006, Gainesville, Florida – Two T-45C Goshawk jets from Training Air Wing One (TW-1) prepare to perform a flyover for football fans at Gator Stadium prior to the start of a University of Florida Gators game. (U.S. Navy photo by 1st Lt. Andrew Straessle)

19 November 2006, Al Oaim, Iraq – With precision-guided AGM-114 Hellfire missiles at the ready, an AH-1W Super Cobra departs to patrol the skies of Western Iraq. (U.S. Marine Corps photo by Cpl. Cullen J. Tiernan)

15 November 2006, Al Asad, Iraq – An F/A-18 Hornet from the "Valions" of VFA-15 take advantage of a larger flight line than the one aboard the USS Theodore Roosevelt (CVN 71). After months of duty at sea, a detachment from VFA-15 recently hit the sand in Al Asad to continue combat operations during the Roosevelt's port call in Dubai. (U.S. Marine Corps photo by Cpl. Micah Snead)

19 November 2006, over North Carolina – The Coast Guard's Long Range Search (LRS) aircraft solution includes six new C-130Js that will be missionized and sixteen legacy HC-130Hs that will be upgraded to ensure their continued performance in the Deepwater system. (U.S. Coast Guard photo courtesy of Northrop Grumman)

22 November 2006, Arabian Sea – Ordnancemen assigned to the "Jolly Rogers" of VFA-103 transport a GBU-12 laser-guided bomb and two GBU-38 GPS-guided bombs to an F/A-18F Super Hornet aboard the USS Dwight D. Eisenhower (CVN 69). (U.S. Navy photo by Mass Communication Specialist 2nd Class Miguel Angel Contreras)

25 November 2006, Arabian Sea – An F/A-18C Hornet assigned to the world-famous "Pukin Dogs" of VFA-143 launches from the USS Dwight D. Eisenhower (CVN 69). Eisenhower and embarked Carrier Air Wing Seven (CVW-7) are on a regularly scheduled deployment in support of Maritime Security Operations. (U.S. Navy photo by Mass Communication Specialist Seaman Apprentice Rafael Figueroa Medina)

25 November 2006, Arabian Sea – A plane director guides an F/A-18C Hornet assigned to the "Wildcats" of VFA-131 on board the USS Dwight D. Eisenhower (CVN 69). (U.S. Navy photo by Mass Communication Specialist Seaman Apprentice Rafael Figueroa Medina)

27 November 2006, Whidbey Island, Washington – Lockheed P-3 Orion maritime patrol aircraft sit on the ramp after a storm dumped four-to-six inches of snow. (U.S. Navy photo by Mass Communication Specialist 1st Class Bruce McVicar)

06 December 2006, Atlantic Ocean – MV-22 Ospreys from squadrons VMM-263 and VMM-162 practiced touch-and-go's aboard the amphibious assault ship USS Wasp (LHD 1) in preparation for future deck landing qualifications. Wasp is in transit to Norfolk, Virginia, after visiting Philadelphia for the Army-Navy football game. (U.S. Navy photo by Mass Communication Specialist 2nd Class Katie Earley)

28 November 2006, Coronado, California – Aviation Structural Mechanic 3rd Class Amanda Fields and Airman Jared Muise from the "Wolfpack" of HSL-45 install a hoist on an SH-60 Seahawk. (U.S. Navy photo by Mass Communication Specialist Seaman Omar A. Dominquez)

29 November 2006, Al Asad, Iraq – A Marine Corps AV-8B Harrier assigned to the "Avengers" of VMA-211 returns from a close air support mission over Iraq. (U.S. Marine Corps photo by Cpl. James B. Hoke)

08 December 2006, Pacific Ocean – Commander, Strike Force Training Pacific, Rear Adm. Gerald R. Beaman, launches in an F/A-18 Super Hornet assigned to the "Black Aces" of VFA-41 aboard the USS Nimitz (CVN 68). Nimitz is currently underway conducting a Composite Training Unit Exercise off the coast of Southern California. (U.S. Navy photo by Mass Communication Specialist 3rd Class Roland Franklin)

29 November 2006, Portsmouth, Virginia – Sailors assigned to the crash and salvage division aboard the USS Harry S. Truman (CVN 75) investigate a simulated fire in a F/A-18 Hornet. Trainers are participating in flight deck drills during a one-day planned fast cruise in preparation for upcoming sea trials. (U.S. Navy photo by Mass Communications Specialist 3rd Class Greg Pierot)

01 December 2006, Atlantic Ocean – A U.S. Coast Guard HH-60 Jayhawk gets a closer look at the fishing vessel "Miss Melissa," as a boat crew deployed from the U.S. Navy's amphibious transport dock ship USS San Antonio (LPD 17) makes their way to the distressed vessel in heavy seas and 40 knot winds. (U.S. Navy photo by Mass Communication Specialist 1st Class Erik Hoffmann)

U.S. Naval Aviation

08 December 2006, Pacific Ocean – Rear Adm. Gerald R. Beaman makes a successful arrested landing in an F/A-18 Super Hornet aboard the USS Nimitz (CVN 68). (U.S. Navy photo by Mass Communication Specialist 3rd Class Roland Franklin)

04 December 2006, Pacific Ocean – An EA-6B Prowler assigned to the "Black Ravens" of VAQ-135 launches from the USS Nimitz (CVN 68) during an exercise off Southern California. (U.S. Navy photo by Mass Communication Specialist 3rd Class Roland Franklin)

06 December 2006, Arabian Sea – Sailors prepare for flight operations aboard the USS Dwight D. Eisenhower (CVN 69) during Maritime Security Operations. (U.S. Navy photo by Mass Communication Specialist Seaman David Danals)

08 December 2006, Pacific Ocean – An E-2C Hawkeye assigned to the "Wallbangers" of VAW-117 prepares to make an arrested landing during flight operations on the USS Nimitz (CVN 68). Nimitz is underway conducting a Composite Training Unit Exercise off the coast of Southern California. (U.S. Navy photo by Mass Communication Specialist 3rd Class Roland Franklin)

13 December 2006, Al Asad, Iraq – Capt. Jacob L. Purdon inspects two laser-guided bombs loaded onto an F/A-18D Hornet assigned to the 3rd Marine Aircraft Wing before a night flight. (U.S. Marine Corps photo by Cpl. Jonathan K. Teslevich)

12 December 2006, Atlantic Ocean – A T-45 Goshawk prepares to launch off of the USS Theodore Roosevelt (CVN 71) during carrier qualifications as part of the fleet response plan. (U.S. Navy photo by Mass Communication Specialist Seaman Sheldon Rowley)

17 December 2006, Atlantic Ocean – Lt. Jarrod Groves prepares to land an MH-60S Seahawk assigned to the "Chargers" of HSC-26 aboard the USS Theodore Roosevelt (CVN 71) during vertical replenishment drills. HSC-26 is home-ported in Norfolk, Virginia. (U.S. Navy photo by Mass Communication Specialist Seaman Zach Hernandez)

19 December 2006, Persian Gulf – An aircraft director signals to an F/A-18C Hornet from the "Wildcats" of VFA-131 prior to launch aboard the USS Dwight D. Eisenhower (CVN 69). (U.S. Navy photo by Mass Communication Specialist Seaman David Danals)

15 December 2006, Atlantic Ocean – A Sikorsky MH-60 Seahawk attached to the "Chargers" of HSC-26 prepares to drop supplies aboard the USS Theodore Roosevelt (CVN 71). HSC-26 transferred supplies from the dry cargo/ammunition ship USNS Lewis and Clark (T-AKE 1) during a vertical replenishment at sea. (U.S. Navy photo by Mass Communication Specialist 1st Class John Mason)